SINGER

SEWING REFERENCE LIBRARY®

Quilt Projects
by Machine

CREATIVE
PUBLISHING
international

CHANHASSEN, MINNESOTA
www.creativepub.com

SINGER

SEWING REFERENCE LIBRARY®

Quilt Projects
by Machine

Contents

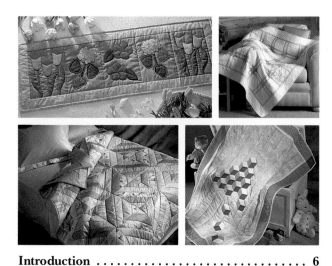

CREATIVE PUBLISHING international

President/CEO: Michael Eleftheriou
Vice President/Publisher: Linda Ball
Vice President/Retail Sales: Kevin Haas

Copyright © 1992
Creative Publishing international, Inc.
18705 Lake Drive East
Chanhassen, Minnesota 55317
1-800-328-3895
www.creativepub.com
All rights reserved

QUILT PROJECTS BY MACHINE
Created by: The Editors of Creative
Publishing international, Inc., in
cooperation with the Sewing Education
Department, Singer Sewing Company.
Singer is a trademark of The Singer
Company Limited and is used under
license.

Books available in this series:
Color and Design on Fabric, The Complete Photo Guide to Sewing, Decorative Machine Stitching,
Designer Projects for Bed & Bath, Fabric Artistry, Embellished Quilted Projects, Halloween Costumes,
The New Quilting by Machine, The New Sewing Essentials, The New Sewing with a Serger, The New
Step-by-Step Home Decorating Projects, Quilted Projects & Garments, The Quilting Bible, Sewing for
Children, Upholstery Basics

Library of Congress
Cataloging-in-Publication Data

Quilt projects by machine.

p. cm – (Singer sewing reference library)
Includes index.
ISBN 0-86573-278-7 (hardcover)
ISBN 0-86573-279-5 (softcover)
1. Patchwork — Patterns. 2. Machine sewing.
3. Patchwork quilts.
I. Creative Publishing international. II. Series.
TT835.Q525   1992
746.9'7 - dc20   92-19930

Executive Editor: Zoe A. Graul
Technical Director: Rita C. Opseth
Project Manager: Joseph Cella
Senior Art Director: Lisa Rosenthal
Writer: Lori Ritter
Editor: Janice Cauley
Sample Coordinator: Carol Olson
Styling Director: Bobbette Destiche
Technical Photo Director: Bridget Haugh
Fabric Editor: Joanne Wawra
Quilt Consultant: Susan Stein
Sewing Staff: Jann Erickson,
   Phyllis Galbraith, Bridget Haugh,
   Sara Macdonald, Linda Neubauer,
   Carol Olson, Carol Pilot,
   Wendy Richardson, Susan Stein,
   Nancy Sundeen, Barb Vik
*Director of Development Planning
   & Production:* Jim Bindas
Production Manager: Amelia Merz
Studio Manager: Cathleen Shannon

Assistant Studio Manager: Rena Tassone
Lead Photographer: John Lauenstein
Photographers: Rebecca Hawthorne,
   Rex Irmen, Bill Lindner,
   Mark Macemon, Paul Najlis,
   Mike Parker
Contributing Photographers: Phil Aarestad,
   Leo Kim, Chuck Nields, Brad Parker
Photo Stylist: Susan Pasqual
Electronic Publishing Specialist: Joe Fahey
Production Staff: Diane Dreon-Krattiger,
   Adam Esco, Eva Hanson, Jim Huntley,
   Phil Juntti, Paul Najlis, Mike Schauer,
   Greg Wallace, Nik Wogstad
Consultants: Ann Fatigati, Pamela Hastings,
   Priscilla Miller, Nancy Raschka,
   Debra Wagner, Donna Wilder
Contributors: Cherrywood Quilts & Fabrics;
   Coats & Clark Inc.; Concord House,
   Division of Concord Fabrics Inc.;
   Dyno Merchandise Corporation;

EZ International; Fairfield Processing
Corporation; HTC-Handler Textile
Corporation; Olfa® Products
International; Salem Rule; Spartex Inc.;
Swiss-Metrosene, Inc.

Printed on American paper by:
R. R. Donnelley
10 9 8 7

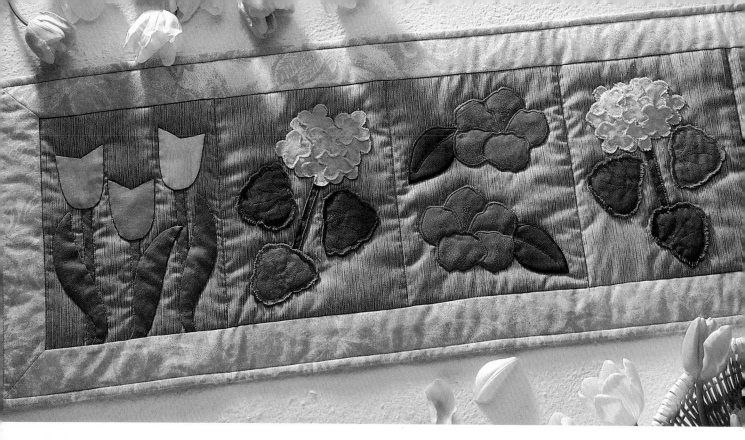

Introduction

Quilting is as popular today as it was years ago. Designing and making quilts is a creative outlet that allows us to express our personal tastes. Quilt designs, some of which are hundreds of years old, continue to be used traditionally and explored in new dimensions.

In *Quilt Projects by Machine,* you can choose from many quilt designs to make wall hangings, bed quilts, lap quilts, and table runners. The projects range from easy-to-sew quilts to others that are more challenging. This book gives you complete instructions, including timesaving construction techniques, for each project. Also included are many ideas for giving traditional designs a variety of new looks.

The Quilt Basics section guides you through the steps of quilt construction, using quick cutting techniques and easy machine methods. It presents the basic sashing and border styles, and helps you calculate yardage for

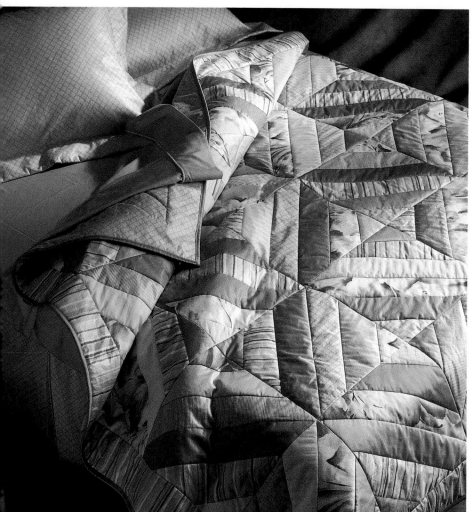

Bed quilt

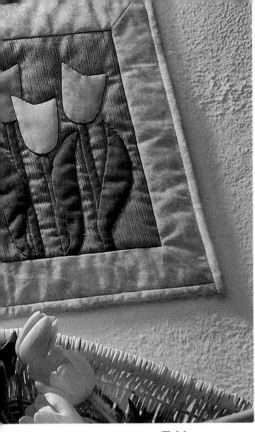

Table runner

Lap quilt or wall hanging

sashing, borders, and binding, should you decide to make your own design changes.

In the Quilt Projects section, you can choose from a variety of projects, from a traditional Pine Trees quilt to a contemporary landscape. We show you how to vary designs by changing the colors or rearranging the blocks, and how to use simplified cutting techniques instead of time-consuming templates. Three methods of appliqué, the blindstiched, frayed, and satin-stitched, are also given.

The Creative Sashing and Borders section includes three quilting projects that feature dominant sashing designs. These designs are quick to sew, using plain or simple quilt blocks. You will also learn how to design creative borders, including an appliquéd border. These border ideas can be used with many of the projects in the book, adding special interest to your quilts.

Baby quilt

Quilt Basics

Fabrics & Batting

Fabric of 100 percent cotton is the best choice for quilt tops and backings. Cotton fabric is easy to work with and is available in a wide range of colors and prints. Cotton/polyester blends may be used, but they tend to pucker when stitched.

Cotton fabrics in hand-dyed gradations of solid colors are convenient for making quilts with subtle blends and mixtures of colors. Hand-dyed cottons are available in packets of eight "fat quarters," which measure about 18" (46 cm) square, in gradations of one color or in a blend of colors. These fabrics can be purchased from quilting stores and mail-order sources.

Nontraditional fabrics, such as decorator fabrics, laces, silks, lamés, old table or bed linens, and garment scraps, may be used for variety. Wall hangings are good projects for fragile fabrics, since the durability of the fabric is less important in wall hangings.

Rinse washable fabrics in warm water to preshrink them and remove any sizing. Check the rinse water of dark or vivid fabrics to be sure they are colorfast; if dye transfers to the water, continue rinsing the fabric until the water is clear. Machine dry the fabric until it is only slightly damp; then press.

Batting is available in several types. Cotton batting gives a flat, traditional appearance when quilted, but requires quilting every 1½" to 2" (3.8 to 5 cm) to prevent the fibers from bunching or shifting. Polyester batting gives a puffy look and is more stable and easier to handle than cotton batting. Cotton/polyester batting combines the flat appearance of cotton with the stability and ease in handling of polyester; it is a versatile batting, suitable for wall hangings, table runners, and bed quilts. Avoid high-loft batting, because it makes machine quilting more difficult.

Batting is available in several types (top to bottom): cotton, polyester, and cotton/polyester blend.

Quilting fabrics are often arranged according to color, making it easier to select the fabrics for a project.

Quick Cutting Techniques

Quick cutting techniques are used for the projects in this book. With the exception of appliqués, all pieces can be cut quickly and accurately using a rotary cutter, cutting mat, and a clear plastic ruler. It is not necessary to straighten quilting fabrics that are off-grain or to find the grainline by pulling threads or tearing the fabric.

All pieces, including borders, sashing, and binding, are cut on the crosswise grain unless otherwise specified. Strips for sashing, borders, and binding are cut after the quilt top is completed, to ensure accurate measurements. Cut strips for the most efficient use of the fabric.

Strips are cut across the width of the fabric; these strips are then cut into the required pieces. Most pieces can be cut using a wide quilting ruler with a marking for a 45° angle. Specialty rulers are available for cutting specific patterns, such as diamonds. Tape thin strips of fine sandpaper across the width of the bottom of see-through rulers, using double-stick tape, to prevent the ruler from slipping when you are cutting fabric.

How to Cut Fabric Using Quick Cutting Techniques

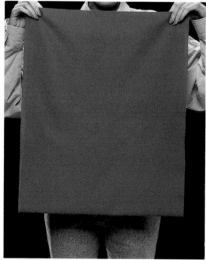

1) Fold the fabric in half, selvages together. Hold the selvage edges, letting fold hang free. Shift one side of the fabric until fold hangs straight. Fold line is on the straight of grain.

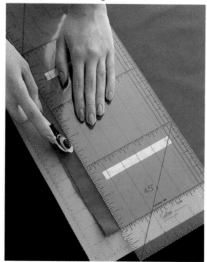

2) Lay fabric on cutting mat, with fold along a grid line. Place ruler on fabric close to raw edge at 90° angle to the fold. Trim along edge of ruler, taking care not to move the fabric.

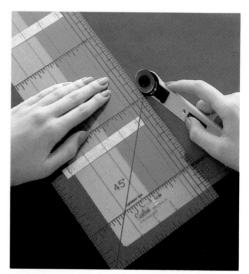

3) Place ruler on fabric, aligning trimmed edge with measurement on ruler; cut along edge of ruler. After cutting several strips, check fabric to be sure cut edge is still at 90° angle to fold, as in step 2.

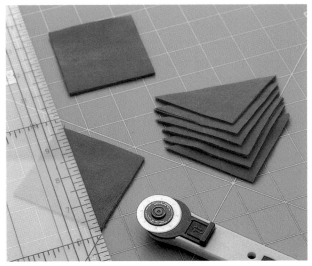

4) Cut squares and rectangles from strips; three or four strips may be stacked with the edges matching exactly. Place the ruler on fabric near selvages at 90° angle to long edges of strips. Trim off selvages. Place ruler on fabric, aligning short edge of fabric with measurement on ruler. Cut, holding ruler firmly.

5) Cut squares into triangles by cutting diagonally through each square; cut once or twice diagonally, following cutting directions for specific project. Three or four squares may be stacked, matching edges exactly.

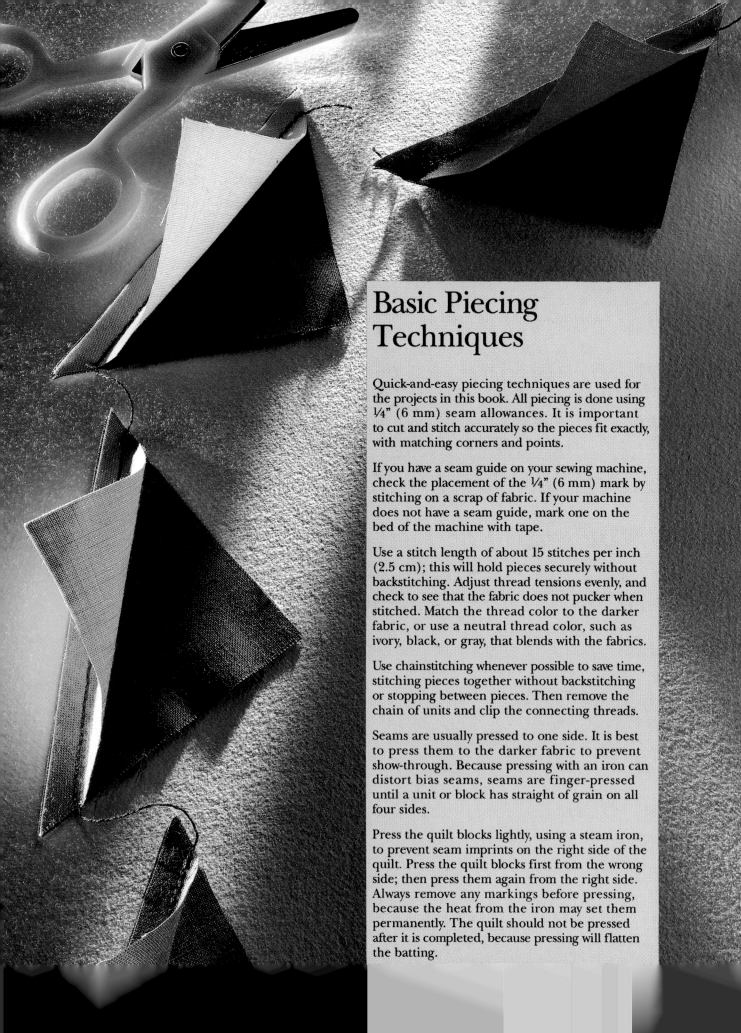

Basic Piecing Techniques

Quick-and-easy piecing techniques are used for the projects in this book. All piecing is done using ¼" (6 mm) seam allowances. It is important to cut and stitch accurately so the pieces fit exactly, with matching corners and points.

If you have a seam guide on your sewing machine, check the placement of the ¼" (6 mm) mark by stitching on a scrap of fabric. If your machine does not have a seam guide, mark one on the bed of the machine with tape.

Use a stitch length of about 15 stitches per inch (2.5 cm); this will hold pieces securely without backstitching. Adjust thread tensions evenly, and check to see that the fabric does not pucker when stitched. Match the thread color to the darker fabric, or use a neutral thread color, such as ivory, black, or gray, that blends with the fabrics.

Use chainstitching whenever possible to save time, stitching pieces together without backstitching or stopping between pieces. Then remove the chain of units and clip the connecting threads.

Seams are usually pressed to one side. It is best to press them to the darker fabric to prevent show-through. Because pressing with an iron can distort bias seams, seams are finger-pressed until a unit or block has straight of grain on all four sides.

Press the quilt blocks lightly, using a steam iron, to prevent seam imprints on the right side of the quilt. Press the quilt blocks first from the wrong side; then press them again from the right side. Always remove any markings before pressing, because the heat from the iron may set them permanently. The quilt should not be pressed after it is completed, because pressing will flatten the batting.

Tips for Piecing

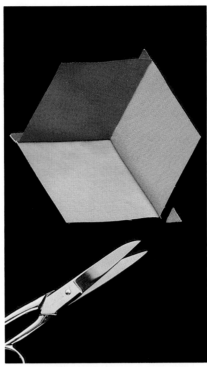

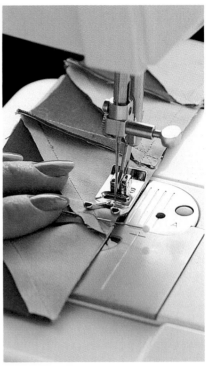

Stitch intersecting seams with the seam allowances finger-pressed in opposite directions, to evenly distribute the bulk.

Trim off any points that extend beyond edges of a unit or block. This eliminates unnecessary bulk and allows for smooth stitching during quilting.

Stitch through the center of the "X" formed by pieced triangles, to make sure the points of the triangles are complete.

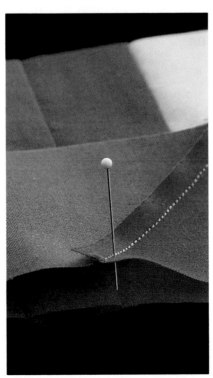

Pin pieces of slightly different lengths together, matching points. Stitch with longer piece on bottom, easing in excess fullness.

Match points by inserting a pin through the points where the seamlines should meet; remove pin before stitching.

Finger-press bias seams to avoid distorting them. Press with an iron only after unit or quilt block has straight of grain on all four sides.

Sashing

Sashing strips separate and frame individual quilt blocks, while they unify a quilt and change its finished size. A quilt top can be made larger by using sashing strips.

a

b

Plain sashing (**a**) is a good choice for a quilt with a complex block design and may be used with a matching border. Short, vertical sashing strips join the blocks into rows, and long, horizontal sashing strips join the rows. Sashing with connecting squares (**b**) adds more interest to a quilt. When this method is used, an outer sashing frames the blocks.

The sashing strips are cut after the quilt blocks are pieced and measured; this allows for any variance in size that may have occurred in seaming. Sashing strips are usually cut on the crosswise grain. If it is necessary to piece long sashing strips, the seam placement is usually planned so the seams are at the center of each strip.

To determine the number of sashing strips required, draw a sketch of the quilt top or arrange the quilt blocks on a large, flat surface. When estimating the yardage for sashing, do not include the selvages. Allow for some shrinkage if the fabric will be prewashed. On the cutting layouts, plan for about 40" (102 cm) of usable width for 45" (115 cm) fabric.

How to Estimate Yardage for Sashing

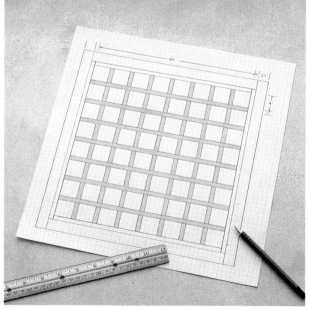

1) Draw a sketch of the quilt top, labeled with the measurements of blocks, borders, and sashing strips; draw seams for sashing on sketch.

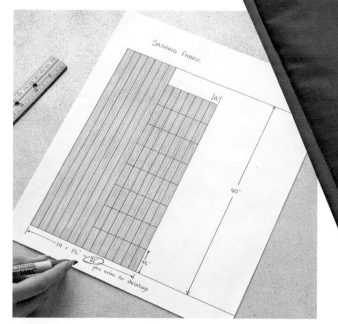

2) Draw cutting layout for sashing strips, labeling usable width of fabric. Sketch sashing strips, including seam allowances, on crosswise or lengthwise grainline, labeling measurements. Add the measurements to estimate yardage.

16

How to Make and Apply Plain Sashing

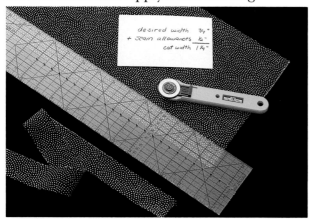

1) Cut sashing strips to the desired width of sashing plus ½" (1.3 cm) for seam allowances.

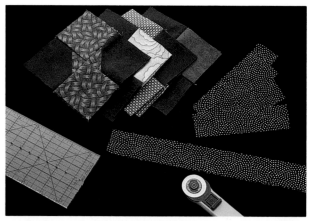

2) Measure sides of several quilt blocks to determine the shortest measurement; cut short sashing strips to this length.

3) Stitch short sashing strips between blocks, right sides together, to form rows; do not stitch strips to ends of rows. Press seam allowances toward sashing.

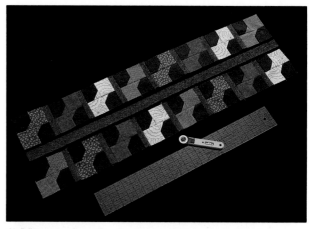

4) Measure length of rows to determine the shortest measurement. Cut the long sashing strips to this length, piecing as necessary.

5) Mark centers of sashing strips and rows. Place one long sashing strip along bottom of one row, right sides together; match and pin centers and ends. Pin along length, easing in any excess fullness; stitch. Repeat for remaining rows, except for bottom row. Press seam allowances toward sashing strips.

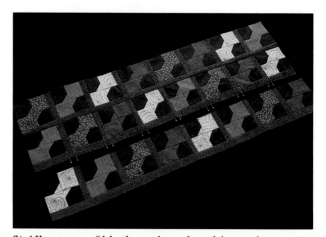

6) Align rows of blocks and mark sashing strips, as shown. Pin bottom of sashing strip to top of next row, right sides together; align marks to seamlines. Stitch as in step 5. Press seam allowances toward sashing. Continue until all rows are joined.

How to Make and Apply Sashing with Connecting Squares

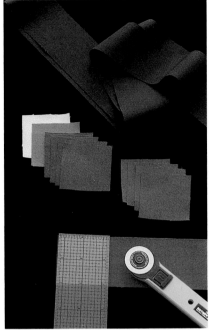

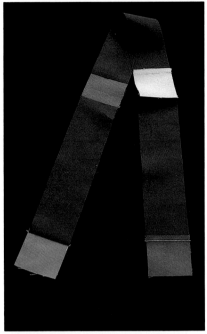

1) Cut strips to desired width of the sashing plus ½" (1.3 cm) for seam allowances. From contrasting fabric, cut connecting squares for corners, with sides of squares equal to cut width of sashing strips.

2) Measure sides of several blocks to determine shortest measurement; cut sashing strips to this length. Stitch strips between blocks, right sides together, to form rows; ease in fullness. Stitch strips to ends of rows. Press seam allowances toward strips.

3) Stitch the remaining sashing strips alternately to connecting squares, to equal the length of the block-and-sashing row; there will be a connecting square at each end. Press seam allowances toward sashing strips.

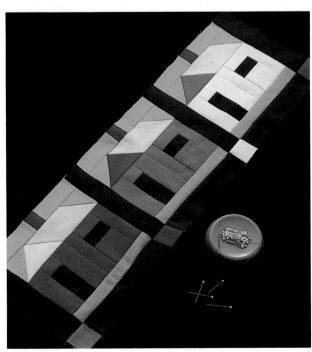

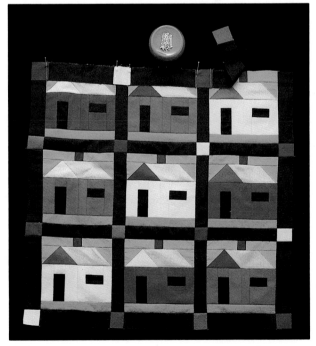

4) Place one sashing unit along the bottom of the first block-and-sashing row, right sides together, matching seams. Pin along length, easing in any fullness; stitch. Repeat for remaining rows.

5) Pin bottom of one sashing unit to top of next row, matching seams, as in step 4; stitch. Press seam allowances toward sashing strip. Continue until all rows are joined. Stitch sashing unit to upper edge.

Borders

A border frames the quilt and visually finishes the edges. The three basic styles of borders are lapped borders, borders with interrupted corners, and mitered borders. In general, a lapped border is used with solid fabrics or all-over prints, and a mitered border is used with striped or border-print fabrics. A border with interrupted corners is suitable with all types of fabrics.

Any of these basic styles can be used as a single or double border. A single border provides a simple frame for the quilt design. A double border can be used to enhance and unify a design by repeating two or more of the colors in the quilt top.

The border strips are cut after the quilt top is pieced and measured, because even the slightest variance in seam allowances can affect the finished size of the quilt top. The cut length of the border strips is determined by measuring through the middle of the quilt; this maintains the overall dimensions of the quilt.

Border strips are usually cut on the crosswise grain and pieced together for the necessary length. If seaming is required, the seam placement may be random; however, the seams should generally not be closer than 12" (30.5 cm) to a corner. For less noticeable seams, piece the strips diagonally. Borders cut from striped fabrics or border prints will usually have to be cut on the lengthwise grainline.

When estimating yardage, do not include selvages. Allow for shrinkage if the fabric will be prewashed; plan for about 40" (102 cm) of usable width on the cutting layouts for 45" (115 cm) fabric.

How to Estimate Yardage for Borders

1) **Draw** a sketch of the quilt top, labeled with measurements of blocks, borders, and sashing strips. Plan placement of border seams, if desired; draw seams on sketch.

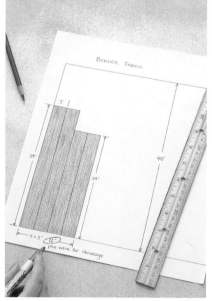

2) **Draw** cutting layout for borders, labeling usable width of fabric. Sketch crosswise or lengthwise border strips, including the seam allowances; label the measurements. Add lengthwise measurements to estimate yardage.

Single borders (above) include: lapped border (**a**), border with interrupted corners (**b**), and mitered border (**c**).

Double borders (left) may be lapped or mitered or have interrupted corners. The inner border is generally narrower than the outer border.

How to Make and Apply a Lapped Border

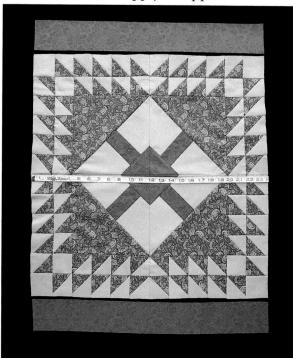

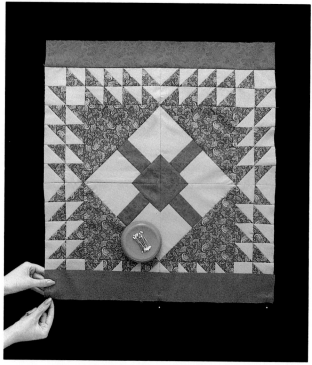

Single border. 1) Measure the quilt top across the middle. Cut two strips equal to this measurement, piecing as necessary; width of strips is equal to finished width of border plus ½" (1.3 cm).

2) Pin strip to upper edge of quilt top at center and ends, right sides together; pin along length, easing in any fullness. Stitch; press seam allowances toward border. Repeat at lower edge.

3) Measure quilt top down the middle, including border strips. Cut two strips as in step 1. Pin and stitch strips to sides of quilt top as in step 2. Press seam allowances toward border.

Double border. Apply inner border, following steps 1 to 3, above. Measure the quilt top across and down the middle, including the inner border; cut and apply the outer border as for inner border.

How to Make and Apply a Border with Interrupted Corners

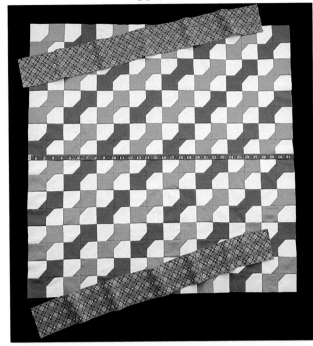

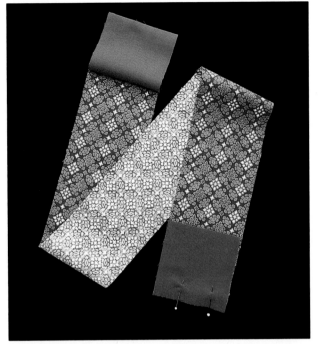

Single border. 1) Measure the quilt top across the middle. Cut two strips equal to this measurement; width of strips is equal to finished width of border plus ½" (1.3 cm). Repeat, measuring the quilt top down the middle from top to bottom.

2) Cut four squares from contrasting fabric, with sides of squares equal to cut width of border strips. Stitch squares, right sides together, to ends of side border strips.

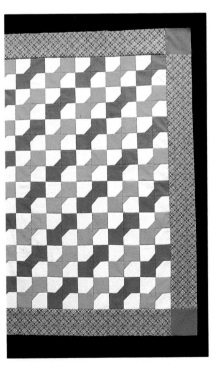

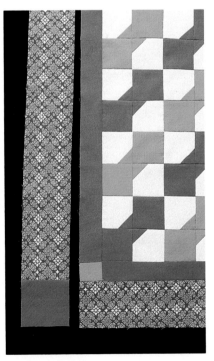

3) Pin upper border strip to upper edge of quilt top at center and ends, right sides together; pin along length, easing in any fullness. Stitch; press seam allowances toward border. Repeat at lower edge.

4) Pin and stitch pieced border strips to sides of quilt top as in step 3, matching seamlines at corners. Press seam allowances toward border.

Double border. Apply the inner border, following steps 1 to 4. Measure the quilt top across and down the middle, including the inner border; cut and apply outer border as for inner border.

How to Make and Apply a Mitered Border

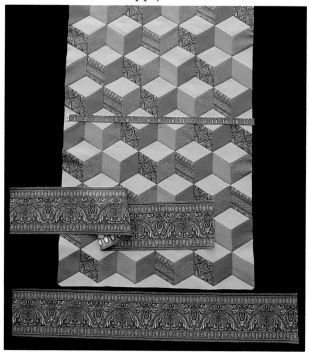

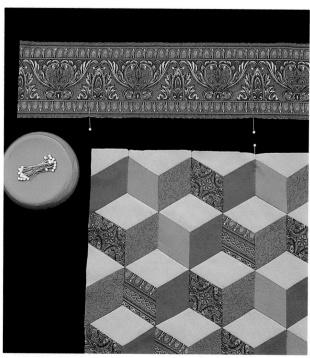

Single border. 1) Measure quilt top across the middle. Cut two strips, with length equal to this measurement plus 2 times finished width of border plus 1" (2.5 cm); cut width is equal to finished width of border plus ½" (1.3 cm). Repeat for side strips, measuring quilt top down the middle from top to bottom.

2) Mark center of quilt top at upper and lower edges; mark center of upper and lower border strips. From each end of border strips, mark the finished width of the border plus ½" (1.3 cm). Place upper border strip on quilt top, right sides together, matching pin marks at center.

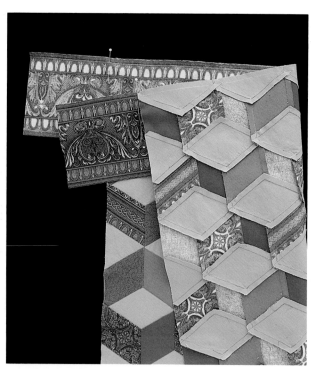

3) Match markings at ends of strip to edges of quilt top; pin. Pin along length, easing in any fullness. Stitch, beginning and ending ¼" (6 mm) from edges of quilt top; backstitch at ends. Repeat at lower edge.

4) Repeat steps 2 and 3 for sides of quilt top.

5) Fold quilt top at corner diagonally, right sides together, matching border seamlines; pin securely. Draw diagonal line on border strip, extending line formed by fold of quilt top.

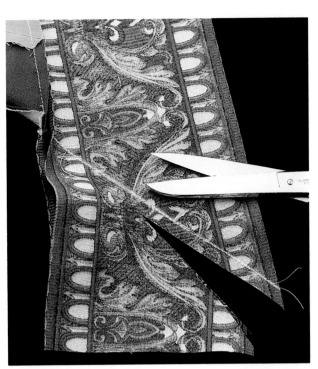

6) Stitch on the marked line; do not catch the seam allowances in stitching. Trim ends of border strips to ¼" (6 mm) seam allowances.

7) Press seam allowances open at corner; press remaining seam allowances toward border strip. Repeat for remaining corners.

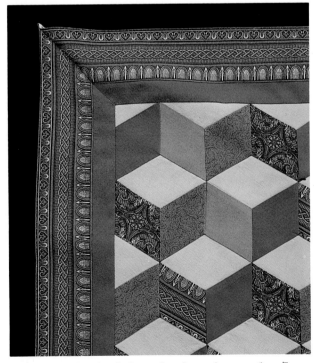

Double border. Apply inner border as in steps 1 to 7. Measure the quilt top across and down the middle, including the inner border; cut and apply outer border as for inner border.

Layering & Basting a Quilt

After the quilt top is completed, the backing and batting are cut, and the three layers are basted together. The backing and batting should extend 2" to 4" (5 to 10 cm) beyond the edges of the quilt top on all sides, for ease in handling.

The yardage for the backing fabric is based on the quilt top measurements and whether or not the backing will be seamed. To add interest to the back of a quilt, piece the backing, using leftover lengths of fabric from the quilt top. When seaming the backing fabric, trim away the selvages before stitching. For larger quilts, you may want to use the backing fabrics available in 90" and 108" (229 and 274.5 cm) widths.

Press the quilt top and backing fabric and mark any quilting design lines (page 30) on the quilt top before layering and basting. If you are using polyester batting, unroll the batting and lay it flat for several hours to allow the wrinkles to smooth out. If you are using cotton/polyester batting, rinse and dry it, following the manufacturer's directions.

Basting is necessary to keep the layers from shifting during the quilting process. Traditionally, quilts were basted using a needle and thread; however, safety-pin basting may be used instead. Lay the quilt flat on a hard surface, such as the floor or a large table, and baste the entire quilt.

If basting with thread, use white cotton thread and a large milliners or darning needle. Use a running stitch about 1" (2.5 cm) long. If basting with safety pins, use rustproof pins.

How to Layer and Baste a Quilt

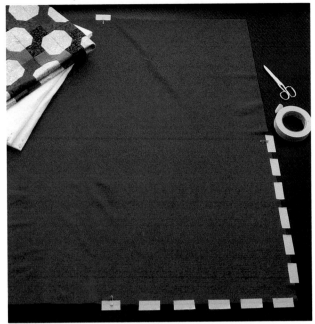

1) Mark the center of each side of the quilt top at raw edges with safety pins; repeat for batting and backing. Tape backing, wrong side up, on the work surface; begin at the center of each side and work toward the corners, stretching fabric slightly. Backing should be taut, but not stretched.

2) Place batting over backing, matching the pins on each side. Smooth, but do not stretch, working from the center of the quilt out to the sides. Place quilt top right side up over batting, matching the pins; smooth, but do not stretch.

3) Baste with safety pins or thread from center of the quilt to pins on sides; if thread-basting, pull stitches snug so layers will not shift, and backstitch at ends. Avoid basting on the marked quilting lines or through the seams. (Both basting methods are shown.)

4) Baste one quarter-section in parallel rows, with saftey pins or thread, about 6" (15 cm) apart, working toward the raw edges. If thread-basting, also baste quarter-section in parallel rows in opposite direction. Repeat for remaining quarter-sections.

5) Remove the tape from backing. Fold edges of backing over batting and edges of quilt top to prevent raw edges of fabric from raveling and to prevent batting from catching on the needle and feed dogs during quilting. Pin-baste.

Stitch-in-the-ditch quilting

Machine-guided outline quilting

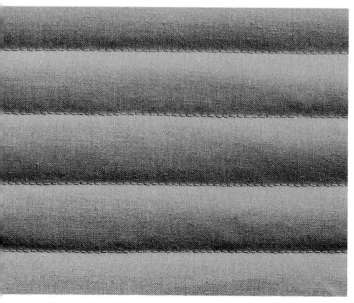

Channel quilting

Quilting Basics

Quilting serves the purpose of holding the layers together and adding surface interest to the quilt. There are two basic types of quilting: machine-guided and free-motion.

Machine-guided Quilting

In machine-guided quilting, the feed dogs and presser foot guide the fabric. This type of quilting is used for stitching long, straight lines or slight curves, and includes stitch-in-the-ditch quilting, outline quilting, and channel quilting.

Stitch-in-the-ditch quilting is the easiest and most commonly used method. It gives definition to blocks, borders, and sashing and is often the only type of quilting needed to complete a project.

Outline quilting is stitched ¼" (6 mm) from the seamlines to emphasize designs. Use machine-guided outline quilting when the project is small enough to allow the quilt to be turned easily. Outline quilting may also be done using free-motion quilting, opposite.

Channel quilting is stitched in evenly spaced lines. The quilting lines may be either diagonal, vertical, or horizontal. Channel quilting provides an easy design to use for borders. Mark the quilting lines, using a straightedge, as on page 30.

Template quilting

Free-motion outline quilting

Free-motion Quilting

In free-motion quilting, the feed dogs are covered or dropped and the fabric is guided by hand, allowing you to stitch in any direction without repositioning the quilt. While there may be some irregularities in the stitches with this method, the overall effect of the quilting is still beautiful. This type of quilting is used to quilt designs with sharp turns and intricate curves, and includes template quilting, outline quilting, and stipple quilting.

Template quilting is used to add designs, such as motifs and continuous border designs, to a quilt. Before quilting, the designs are marked on the fabric, using templates as a guide. Generally, free-motion stitching is used for template quilting; some designs, such as cables with gentle curves, may be quilted using machine-guided stitching. Mark the designs as on page 30.

Free-motion outline quilting is easier than machine-guided for lines of stitching that frequently change direction, as in small squares or triangles. By stitching ¼" (6 mm) from the seamlines, the design lines are emphasized.

Stipple quilting is used to fill in the background. It adds uniform texture to a section of the quilt. Because stipple quilting flattens the area, it can also serve to make other sections of the quilt more prominent.

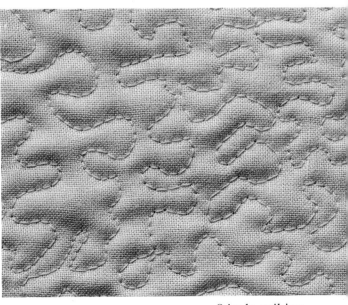

Stipple quilting

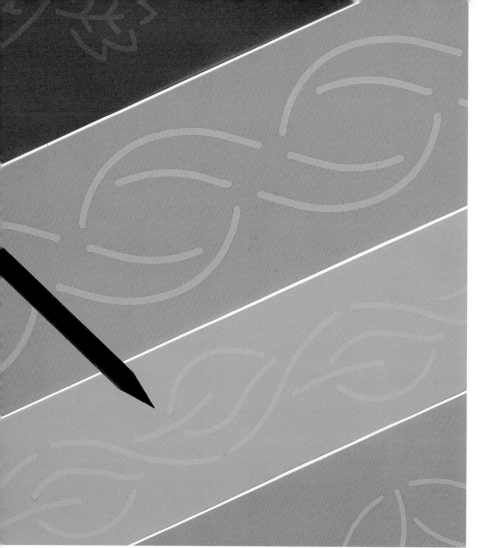

Marking the Quilt

Plan the quilting design to cover the quilt top uniformly. For best results, avoid quilting some areas more heavily than others.

Mark any quilting lines that do not follow seamlines or appliqués, such as those for channel quilting and template quilting. Mark the quilt top before the layers are basted, using a marking pencil intended for quilting; test the marking pencil to be sure the marks can be removed from the fabric. Avoid using water-soluble marking pens, because the entire quilt must be rinsed thoroughly to completely remove the markings.

Templates are used for accurately marking intricate quilting lines.

How to Mark a Quilting Design

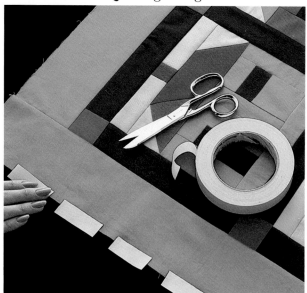

1) **Press** quilt top; place on hard, flat work surface, with corners squared and sides parallel. Tape securely, keeping quilt top smooth and taut.

2) **Mark** quilting design, using a straightedge or template as a guide, beginning at corners of quilt. Mark thin lines, using light pressure. For continuous designs, adjust the length of several motifs slightly to achieve the correct length.

Getting Ready to Quilt

Before you start to quilt, a few simple preparations will make the quilting process easier. Everything from the set-up of the sewing machine and work space to the quilting sequence contributes to the ease and quality of the quilting.

Sewing Machine Preparation

Set up the sewing machine in an area where the quilt will be supported both to the left of and behind the machine. Do not allow the quilt to hang over the back or side of the sewing table; this will cause the quilt to feed through the machine unevenly, resulting in an uneven stitch length.

For machine-guided quilting, attach an Even Feed™ foot, or walking foot, if one is available; this type of presser foot helps to prevent puckering. Use a stitch length of 8 to 10 stitches per inch (2.5 cm).

For free-motion quilting, set the machine for a straight stitch and use a straight-stitch needle plate; cover the feed dogs or lower them. Remove the regular presser foot and, if desired, attach a darning foot. It is not necessary to adjust the stitch length setting on the machine, because the stitch length is determined by a combination of the movement of the quilt and the speed of the needle.

Thread the machine with cotton or monofilament nylon thread. With either thread type, loosen the needle thread tension, if necessary, so the bobbin thread does not show on the right side.

Cotton thread is traditionally used for quilting. Select the thread color according to how much you want the stitching to show. Frequently one thread color that blends with the fabrics in the quilt is used throughout.

Monofilament nylon thread is now popular for machine quilting, because with this thread type, it is usually not necessary to change thread colors. Choose the clear for most fabric colors and the smoke for dark fabrics. The nylon thread is used only in the needle, and a cotton thread is used in the bobbin.

The Quilting Sequence

Plan the sequence of the quilting before you begin to stitch. The sequence varies with the style of the quilt. Generally, begin anchoring the quilt horizontally and vertically by stitching in the ditch of a seamline near the center, then anchoring any borders. This prevents the layers from shifting. Next, stitch along any sashing strips or between blocks, starting in the center and working toward the sides. Once the quilt has been anchored into sections, quilt the areas within the blocks and borders.

Stitching & Handling Tips

Stitch continuously, with as few starts and stops as possible. Check for any tucks in the backing by feeling through the layers of the quilt ahead of the sewing machine needle. Prevent the tucks from being stitched by continuously easing in the excess fabric before it reaches the needle. If a tuck does occur, release the stitches for 3" (7.5 cm) or more, and restitch, easing in excess fabric.

Small projects are easily maneuvered as you machine-quilt. Before quilting larger projects, roll up one side of the quilt to allow it to fit on the sewing machine bed. If the sewing surface is not large enough to hold the remaining width, roll up both sides of the quilt.

How to Quilt a Basic Project

1) Roll one or both sides of the quilt to within 3" (7.5 cm) of the first vertical quilting line to be stitched; this is usually a seamline near the center. If necessary, secure the roll with bicycle pants clips or large safety pins.

2) Hold quilt over shoulder or in lap. Stitch along first quilting line, using stitch-in-the-ditch method (pages 34 and 35); allow the quilt to feed evenly into the machine as you sew. Secure thread tails, opposite.

3) Reroll the quilt to within 3" (7.5 cm) of the first horizontal quilting line to be stitched; this is usually a seamline near the center. Secure with bicycle pants clips or large safety pins. Stitch as in step 2.

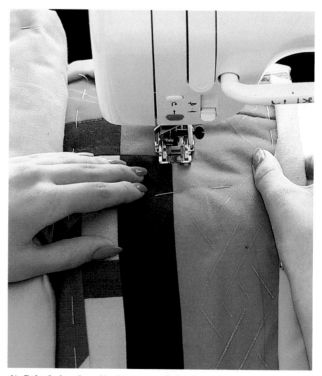

4) Stitch in the ditch around the border; roll quilt as necessary for proper support on table.

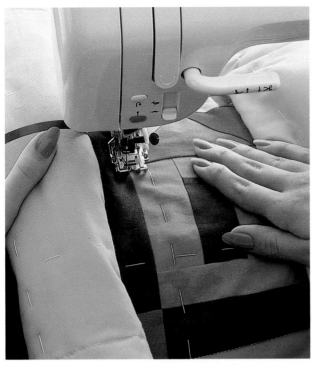

5) Stitch in the ditch along any vertical sashing strips or between blocks, starting near center and working toward sides; roll the quilt as necessary. Repeat for horizontal seamlines.

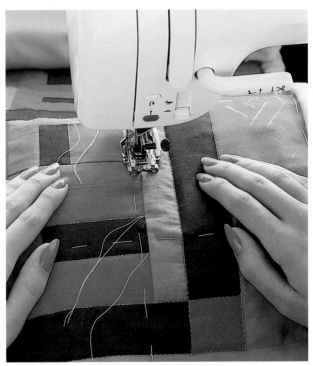

6) Quilt the areas within the blocks and borders, using desired quilting technique (pages 34 and 35).

How to Secure the Thread Tails

1) Draw up the bobbin thread to the quilt top, by turning flywheel by hand and stopping with needle at highest position. Pull on needle thread to bring the bobbin thread up through fabric.

2) Stitch several short stitches to secure threads at the beginning of stitching line, gradually increasing stitch length for about ½" (1.3 cm) to desired length. Reverse procedure at end of stitching.

Quilting Techniques

Machine-guided quilting. Stitch with your hands positioned on either side of the presser foot, holding the fabric taut.

Free-motion quilting. Stitch with your hands positioned so they act as an embroidery hoop, applying gentle tension on the fabric.

For machine-guided quilting, such as stitch-in-the-ditch, outline, and channel quilting, position your hands on either side of the presser foot. Gently press down and hold the fabric taut to prevent the layers from shifting, which would cause puckers or tucks. Ease any excess fabric under the presser foot as you stitch. The presser foot and feed dogs guide the quilt through the machine.

For free-motion quilting, such as template, outline, and stipple quilting, position your hands so they act as an embroidery hoop, and apply gentle tension on the fabric. With the feed dogs covered or lowered and with the presser foot lifter in the lowered position, stitch, moving the fabric with wrist and hand movements. Maintain a steady rhythm and speed as you stitch, to keep the stitch length uniform. When changing your hand positions, stop stitching with the needle down in the fabric.

Type of presser foot depends on the quilting technique used. An Even-Feed™ foot (right) may be used instead of a general-purpose foot for machine-guided quilting. Free-motion quilting is frequently done without using a presser foot, but a darning foot (left) is helpful.

How to Quilt Using Machine-guided Techniques

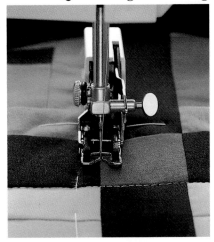

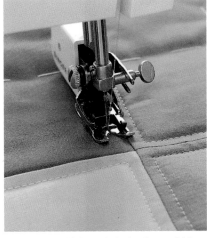

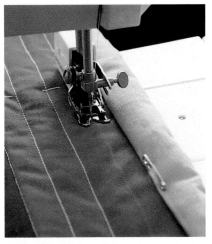

Stitch-in-the-ditch quilting. Stitch over the seamline, stitching in the well of the seam.

Outline quilting. Stitch about ¼" (6 mm) from the seamline, starting at the corner.

Channel quilting. Stitch on marked quilting lines, starting with inner line and working toward edge.

How to Quilt Using Free-motion Techniques

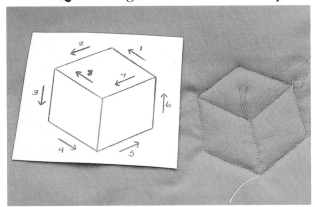

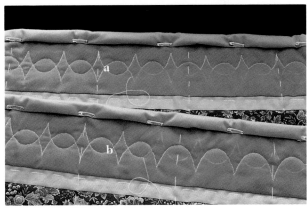

Single-motif template quilting. Determine the longest continuous stitching line possible; stitch. Stitch additional design lines as necessary.

Continuous-motif template quilting. Stitch motifs along one side to points where motifs connect (**a**). Or stitch one side of first motif, then opposite side of second motif, and repeat (**b**). Return to starting point; stitch motifs on opposite side.

Outline quilting. Stitch about ¼" (6 mm) from the seamline, starting at the corner.

Stipple quilting. Stitch random, curving lines. Work in small sections, keeping spaces between quilting lines close; do not cross over lines. Work from edges toward center, covering background uniformly.

Binding a Quilt

Double binding, which is cut on the straight of grain, provides a durable finished edge for a quilt. It can be cut to match the border or cut from a coordinating fabric.

Two finished widths are popular for double binding: regular binding in a scant ½" (1.3 cm) finished width and narrow binding in a scant ⅜" (1 cm). Regular binding is used for most quilts; cut the binding strips 2½" (6.5 cm) wide. Narrow binding is used for small quilts, such as wall hangings 36" (91.5 cm) or smaller; cut the binding strips 2" (5 cm) wide.

The binding strips are cut on the crosswise grain of the fabric and pieced to the necessary length. To determine the yardage for binding, measure the outer edges of the quilt top. Add the measurements together, and add 8" (30 cm); also allow extra length for seam allowances if you are piecing the strips. Divide this number by 40" (102 cm), which is the usable fabric width, and then multiply by the cut width of the binding.

How to Bind a Quilt with Double Binding

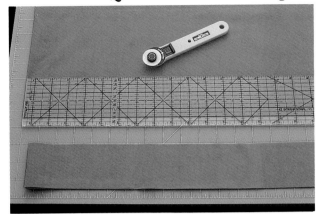

1) **Fold** fabric in half on lengthwise grain (page 12). On the crosswise grain, cut strips 2½" (6.5 cm) wide for regular binding or 2" (5 cm) wide for narrow binding.

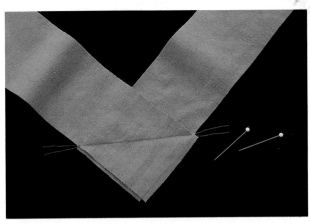

2) **Pin** strips, right sides together, at right angles, if it is necessary to piece the binding strips; strips will form a "V." Stitch diagonally across strips.

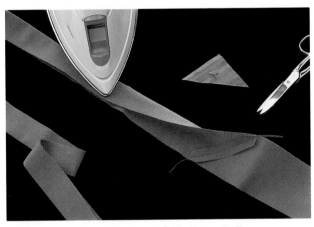

3) **Trim** seam allowances to ¼" (6 mm). Press seam open. Trim points even with edges. Press binding strip in half lengthwise, wrong sides together.

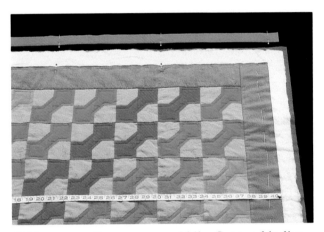

4) **Measure** quilt top across middle. Cut two binding strips equal to this measurement plus 2" (5 cm). Mark binding strips 1" (2.5 cm) from ends; divide area between pins in fourths, and pin-mark. Divide upper and lower edges of quilt in fourths; pin-mark.

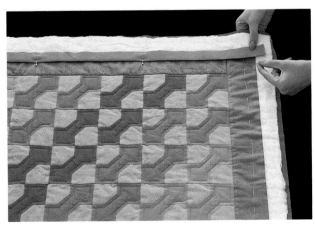

5) **Place** binding strip on upper edge of quilt top, matching raw edges and pin marks; binding will extend 1" (2.5 cm) beyond quilt top at each end. Pin binding along length, easing in any fullness.

6) **Stitch** binding strip to quilt, a scant ¼" (6 mm) from raw edges of binding.

(Continued on next page)

How to Bind a Quilt with Double Binding (continued)

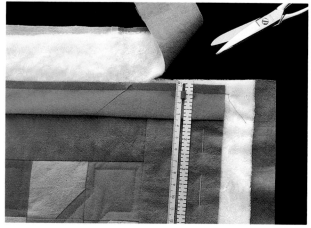

7) Trim excess batting and backing to a scant ½" (1.3 cm) from stitching for regular binding; trim to a scant ⅜" (1 cm) for narrow binding.

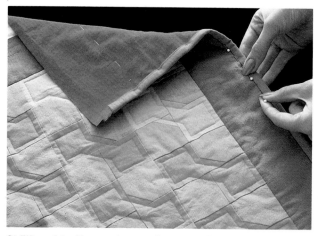

8) Wrap binding strip snugly around edge of quilt, covering stitching line on back of quilt; pin in the ditch of the seam.

9) Stitch in the ditch on right side of quilt, catching binding on back of quilt; for less noticeable stitches, use monofilament nylon thread in the needle.

10) Repeat steps 5 to 9 for lower edge of quilt. Trim ends of upper and lower binding strips even with edges of quilt top.

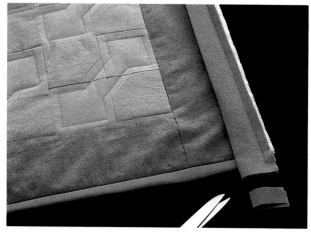

11) Repeat steps 4 to 7 for sides of quilt, measuring quilt top down the middle in step 4. Trim ends of binding strips to extend ½" (1.3 cm) beyond the finished edges of the quilt.

12) Fold binding along the stitching line. Fold ½" (1.3 cm) end of binding over finished edge; press in place. Wrap binding around edge, and stitch in the ditch as in steps 8 and 9. Slipstitch end.

Hanging a Quilt

For a quilt to be displayed as a wall hanging, the weight of the quilt must be distributed evenly. Attach a fabric sleeve to the back of the quilt and insert a wooden lattice that has been sealed with varnish, polyurethane, or paint. To prevent fading or fabric deterioration, display quilts away from direct sunlight or bright, constant artificial light and vacuum them occasionally.

How to Hang a Quilt Using a Fabric Sleeve

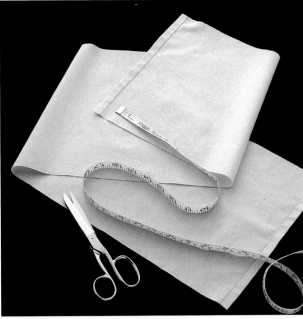

1) **Cut** a piece of washed, unbleached muslin 10" (25.5 cm) wide by the width of the quilt. Turn under and stitch ½" (1.3 cm) double-fold hems at short ends.

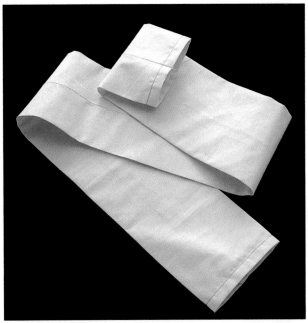

2) **Stitch** long edges of strip, right sides together, in ½" (1.3 cm) seam; press seam allowances open. Turn sleeve right side out; press flat, centering seam.

3) **Pin** the sleeve to the back of the quilt, close to edges. Hand-stitch sleeve to quilt along upper and lower edges; stitch through backing and into batting.

4) **Cut** a wooden lattice ½" (1.3 cm) shorter than width of quilt; insert lattice through sleeve. Secure lattice to wall, placing screws or nails at ends of lattice.

Quilt Projects

Pine Trees

The Pine Trees design is a popular motif for wall hangings. The blocks can be arranged in several ways for a variety of looks.

The grid-piecing method (page 44) is used to piece the *triangle-squares* in the Pine Trees quilt block, allowing you to cut and piece them in one easy operation; a triangle-square is two triangles stitched together on their longest sides to form a square. This grid-piecing method may be used for any quilt that has several triangle-squares.

For easier construction, the tree trunk and base at the corner of the quilt block is made from rectangles, then trimmed to the correct size after piecing.

The instructions that follow are for a wall hanging made from four 12" (30.5 cm) quilt blocks. The finished quilt measures about 24" (61 cm) square.

✂ Cutting Directions

Cut one 18" (46 cm) square from background fabric and one from tree fabric to be used for grid-pieced triangle-squares (**A**). Cut two 8⅞" (22.8 cm) squares from tree fabric; cut squares diagonally into triangles (**B**). Cut eight 2½" (6.5 cm) squares (**C**) and eight 4" × 5½" (10 × 14 cm) rectangles (**D**) from background fabric. Cut four 2" × 4" (5 × 10 cm) rectangles (**E**) and four 3" × 5" (7.5 × 12.5 cm) rectangles (**F**) from trunk fabric.

YOU WILL NEED

½ yd. (0.5 m) fabric for the top of the tree.

½ yd. (0.5 m) fabric for the background.

¼ yd. (0.25 m) fabric for the tree trunk.

¾ yd. (0.7 m) fabric for the backing.

⅜ yd. (0.35 m) fabric for the binding.

Batting, about 28" (71 cm) square.

Block Arrangements

Sawtooth effect is created by arranging the blocks with the tops of the trees toward the center of the quilt.

Starburst effect is created by arranging the blocks with the trunks of the trees toward the center of the quilt.

How to Make Triangle-squares Using the Grid-piecing Method

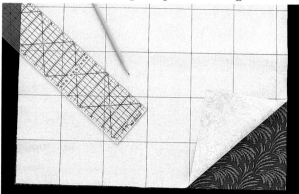

1) Cut one square or rectangle from each of two different fabrics. Draw grid of squares on wrong side of lighter-colored fabric, making the grid squares 7⁄8" (2.2 cm) larger than finished triangle-square; each square of grid makes two triangle-squares.

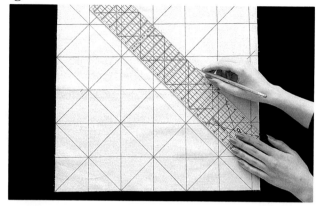

2) Draw diagonal lines through the grid as shown. Draw diagonal lines through grid in opposite direction as shown; there will be one diagonal line through each square.

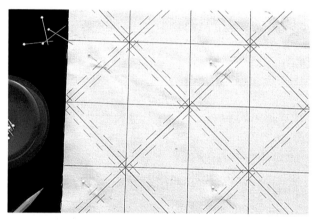

3) Mark dotted stitching lines 1⁄4" (6 mm) from both sides of all diagonal lines. Pin the fabric layers, right sides together.

4) Stitch on all dotted lines. Cut on all solid lines to make triangle-squares. Press seam allowances toward darker fabric. Trim points extending beyond edges of triangle-squares.

How to Make a Pine Trees Wall Hanging

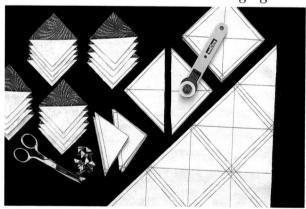

1) Make 72 triangle-squares from 18" (46 cm) squares of fabric, following steps 1 to 4, above; in step 1, draw a grid of 2⁄8" (7.2 cm) squares, six across and six down.

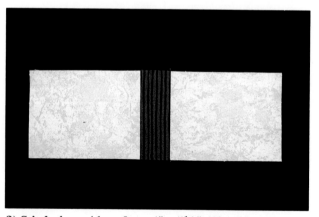

2) Stitch short sides of two 4" × 5½" (10 × 14 cm) rectangles cut from background fabric to long sides of 2" × 4" (5 × 10 cm) rectangle cut for tree trunk, with right sides together and raw edges even.

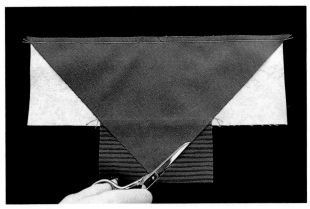

3) Stitch one long edge of 3" × 5" (7.5 × 12.5 cm) rectangle for tree base to one long edge of pieced rectangles, right sides together; match centers of rectangles. Press seam allowances toward tree base.

4) Stitch the large triangle cut from tree fabric to the opposite edge of the trunk unit, with right sides together and raw edges even. Trim the excess background and trunk fabrics to match the triangle. Press seam allowances toward darker fabric.

5) Stitch two rows of four triangle-squares as shown. Stitch rows together; attach to large triangle as shown.

6) Stitch two rows of triangle-squares and two background squares as shown. Stitch rows together; attach to opposite side of triangle, positioning background squares at top of tree.

7) Repeat steps 2 to 6 to make three more blocks. Arrange blocks as desired. Stitch blocks together to form two rows; stitch the rows together. Press quilt top.

8) Cut backing 28" (71 cm) square; press. Layer and baste quilt top, batting, and backing (pages 26 and 27).

9) Quilt (pages 28 to 35). Cut and apply binding (page 37); cut width of binding is 2½" (6.5 cm). Attach fabric sleeve (page 39); to hang quilt on point, attach second sleeve to adjacent side.

More Pine Trees Designs

Corner triangles may be added to the sides of each tree in a Pine Trees quilt, as shown above, setting the trees vertically and making 17" (43 cm) quilt blocks. To cut the triangles for the corners, cut 9⅜" (24 cm) squares from four fabrics in half diagonally; one triangle of each color is used for each block.

The quilt above has 16 blocks, four across and four down. With a 4" (10 cm) border, the finished quilt measures about 76" (193 cm) square, a size suitable for a bed quilt.

The Pine Trees design is fun to make in seasonal colors. Make one with a Christmas theme, or change the colors for a spring, summer, fall, or winter quilt. Combine the seasonal blocks for a four-season quilt that can be displayed year-round.

Even though this design is called Pine Trees, it need not resemble trees at all. With the use of unexpected colors and a block arrangement that radiates out from the center, a four-block quilt can create a colorful starburst effect.

Seasonal theme (left) can be created by using different fabrics for each block. Sashing (pages 16 to 18) has been added to set the blocks apart, and a lapped border (pages 20 to 22) frames the quilt. To make the 18 triangle-squares necessary for each block, use the grid-piecing method on page 44, marking the 2⅞" (7.2 cm) grid, three across and three down, on 9" (23 cm) square of fabric.

Starburst effect (right) is created by the arrangement of the blocks and by using nontraditional colors. For the 16 triangle-squares of the inner rows, mark the 2⅞" (7.2 cm) grid, four across and four down, on 12" (30.5 cm) square of fabric. For the 20 triangle-squares of the outer rows, mark the 2⅞" (7.2 cm) grid, five across and four down, on 15" × 12" (38 × 30.5 cm) rectangle of fabric.

Holiday fabrics (left) can make a festive wall hanging for the Christmas season. A lapped border (pages 20 to 22) frames the quilt. The triangle-squares are grid-pieced as for the quilt with a starburst effect, above.

Bow Ties

Bow Ties is a versatile quilt design that lends itself to many block arrangements. The Bow Ties design is shown here in four different arrangements. In the traditional pattern (opposite), the blocks are arranged in rows, with each bow tie facing in the same direction. As shown in the quilts below, the blocks may also be turned alternately for a zigzag pattern, arranged in units of four blocks for an octagonal pattern, or arranged in a staggered pattern.

Traditionally, templates were used to make a Bow Ties quilt. But this design can now be made using a simplified method that enables quick cutting and chainstitching. The easy method for constructing a single Bow Ties block is on page 50. To make enough blocks for an entire quilt, construct them quickly and efficiently, using chainstitching.

The instructions that follow are for a wall hanging made from sixty-four 4" (10 cm) quilt blocks. The finished quilt measures about 37" (94 cm) square.

✂ Cutting Directions
Each block requires two 2½" (6.5 cm) squares (A) from background fabric and two 2½" (6.5 cm)

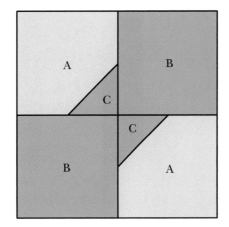

squares (B) from bow-tie fabric, cut from 2½" (6.5 cm) fabric strips. Each block also requires two 1½" (3.8 cm) squares from bow-tie fabric, which will be pieced and trimmed to make triangles (C); cut the 1½" (3.8 cm) squares from 1½" (3.8 cm) fabric strips.

The Bow Ties project requires 16 blocks of each bow-tie color. Cut eight 2½" (6.5 cm) strips from background fabric, cutting each strip into squares to make 128 background squares. Cut two 2½" (6.5 cm) strips from each of four bow-tie fabrics, cutting each strip into squares to make 32 squares from each fabric. Cut two 1½" (3.8 cm) strips from each bow-tie fabric, cutting each strip to make 32 squares from each fabric.

YOU WILL NEED

⅜ yd. (0.35 m) fabric in each of four colors for bow ties.

¾ yd. (0.7 m) fabric for background.

¾ yd. (0.7 m) fabric for border and binding.

1¼ yd. (1.15 m) fabric for backing.

Batting, about 41" (104 cm) square.

Block Arrangements

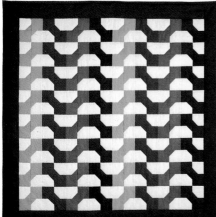

Zigzag pattern has the quilt blocks turned in alternate directions.

Octagonal pattern is created by arranging the quilt blocks in units of four.

Staggered pattern of quilt blocks forms diagonal rows.

How to Make a Bow Ties Quilt Block

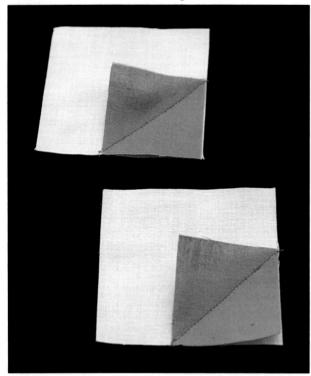

1) Place 1½" (3.8 cm) square in one corner of a background square, with right sides together and raw edges even. Stitch diagonally from corner to corner as shown. Repeat for a second pieced square.

2) Press small square in half along stitched line, matching outer edges to large square. Trim fabric at stitched corner, leaving ¼" (6 mm) seam allowance. Repeat for second pieced square.

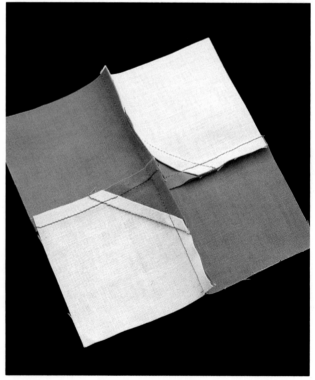

3) Stitch each pieced square to one square from bow-tie fabric, as shown, to make two half-block units.

4) Stitch two units together to form a bow tie, finger-pressing center seam allowances in opposite directions.

How to Make a Bow Ties Quilt

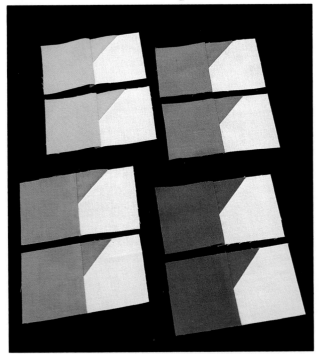

1) Piece blocks for each color, following steps 1 to 4, opposite; for staggered pattern (page 49), construct two half-block units of each color, following steps 1 to 3, opposite.

2) Arrange blocks, eight across and eight down, as shown in the quilts on pages 48 and 49. For staggered pattern, use half-block units to complete design.

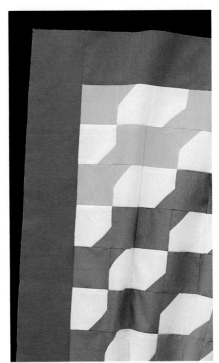

3) Stitch the blocks into rows; stitch rows together, finger-pressing seam allowances in opposite directions. Press quilt top. Cut and attach border strips (pages 20 to 25); cut width of border strips is 3" (7.5 cm).

4) Cut backing 4" (10 cm) larger than quilt top; press. Layer and baste the quilt top, batting, and backing (pages 26 and 27).

5) Quilt (pages 28 to 35). Cut and apply binding (page 37); cut width of binding is 2½" (6.5 cm). For wall hanging, attach fabric sleeve (page 39).

More Bow Ties Designs

The fabric and color selection can dramatically change the look of a Bow Ties quilt. Fabrics that resemble those used in men's neckties give an authentic look. Colors in the Amish tradition have a more striking effect, and subtle variations of gradated colors result in a more subdued quilt. Add variety to a Bow Ties quilt by choosing fabric scraps with different colors and textures for each block.

Many cotton prints resembling necktie fabrics give this Bow Ties quilt a traditional menswear look. An old-fashioned plaid fabric is used for the background of the quilt.

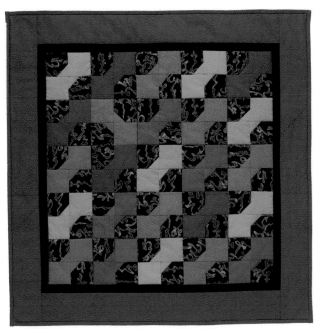

Amish colors used in the traditional pattern create a wall hanging with heirloom appeal. In the Amish tradition of intentionally making the quilt imperfect, one quilt block has been turned in the opposite direction, adding an interesting design element.

Gradations of warm colors are used to achieve a soft look. Make a sketch of the quilt to determine how many blocks of each color you will need.

Scraps can be used to create an eclectic look, with muslin used for the background squares. The octagonal pattern is interrupted with narrow sashing strips.

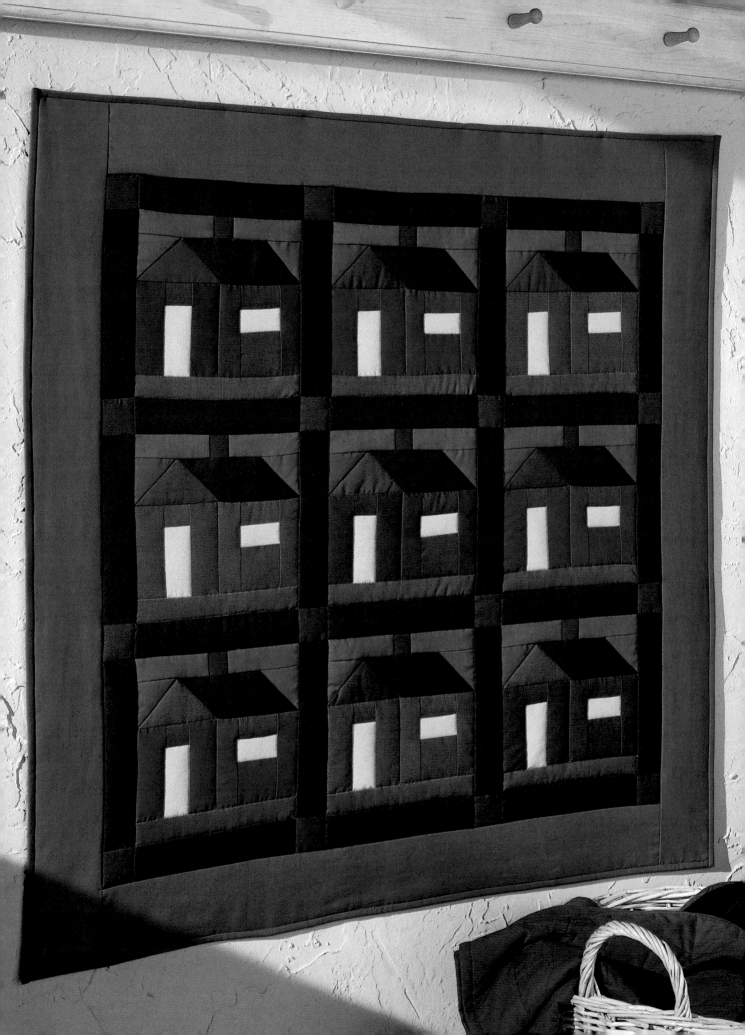

Houses

Pieced picture quilts depicting houses were first developed in the 1800s. They remain popular today because of the versatility of the design. This version of a traditional house block is also quick and easy to cut and piece.

By varying the use of color, you can create a nighttime effect, as shown opposite, using dark fabrics for the houses and sky, and yellow to illuminate the windows and doors. Or create a daytime effect, using bright colors for the houses and black for the windows and doors, as shown in the quilt on page 59.

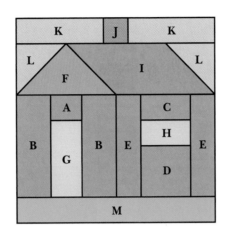

The instructions that follow are for a wall hanging made from nine 8" (20.5 cm) quilt blocks. Sashing with interrupted corners frames the blocks and unifies the overall design. The finished quilt with a single lapped border measures about 36" (91.5 cm) square.

✄ Cutting Directions

Cut the correct number of pieces for each of nine quilt blocks, using the dimensions in the chart below. From each of the three house fabrics, cut enough house and gable pieces for three quilt blocks, making enough for a total of nine blocks.

Pieces to Cut for Each Quilt Block

	Pieces	Number and Size
House	A	One 1½" × 1¾" (3.8 × 4.5 cm) rectangle.
	B	Two 1⅞" × 4½" (4.7 × 11.5 cm) rectangles.
	C	One 1½" × 2½" (3.8 × 6.5 cm) rectangle.
	D	One 2½" (6.5 cm) square.
	E	Two 1½" × 4½" (3.8 × 11.5 cm) rectangles.
Gable	F	One 5¼" (13.2 cm) square, cut diagonally in both directions; use one triangle for each quilt block.
Door	G	One 1¾" × 3½" (4.5 × 9 cm) rectangle.
Window	H	One 1½" × 2½" (3.8 × 6.5 cm) rectangle.
Roof	I	One parallelogram (page 56), cut from 2½" (6.5 cm) strip.
Chimney	J	One 1½" (3.8 cm) square.
Sky	K	Two 1½" × 4" (3.8 × 10 cm) rectangles.
	L	One 2⅞" (7.2 cm) square, cut in half diagonally for two triangles.
Ground	M	One 1½" × 8½" (3.8 × 21.8 cm) rectangle.

YOU WILL NEED

⅜ yd. (0.35 m) fabric in each of three colors for houses and gables.

⅛ yd. (0.15 m) fabric for doors and windows.

⅛ yd. (0.15 m) fabric for roofs.

⅛ yd. (0.15 m) fabric or scraps in each color for chimneys, sky, and ground.

⅓ yd. (0.32 m) fabric for 1½" (3.8 cm) sashing.

½ yd. (0.5 m) fabric for 3" (7.5 cm) border.

⅓ yd. (0.32 m) fabric for binding.

1⅛ yd. (1.05 m) fabric for backing.

Batting, about 40" (102 cm) square.

How to Make a Houses Quilt

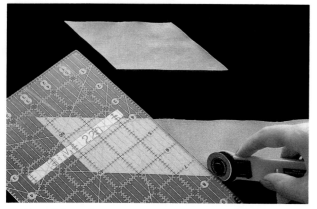

1) Cut 45° angle on one end of fabric strip for roof. Place 3¼" (8.2 cm) mark on ruler along angle-cut; cut strip to make parallelogram. Repeat for eight more roof pieces.

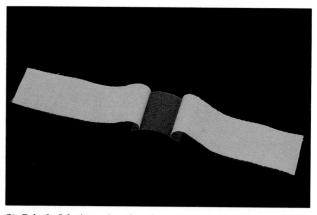

2) Stitch fabric strips for the sky to each side of the chimney piece.

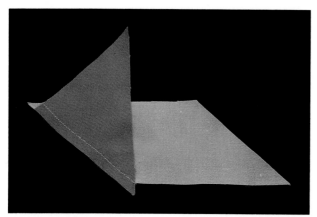

3) Stitch gable piece to roof piece as shown; use a gable color that will contrast with the house color. Finger-press seam allowance toward roof.

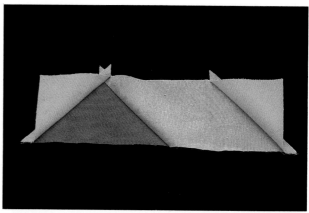

4) Stitch long edge of one sky triangle to one side of roof; stitch long edge of second sky triangle to gable. Finger-press seam allowances toward sky. Trim points extending beyond edges of unit.

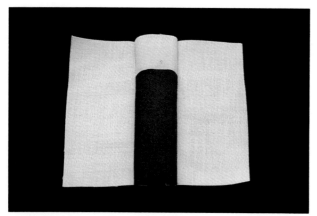

5) Stitch 1½" × 1¾" (3.8 × 4.5 cm) rectangle of house fabric to top of door. Stitch one 1⅞" × 4½" (4.7 × 11.5 cm) rectangle of house fabric to each side of pieced door section as shown.

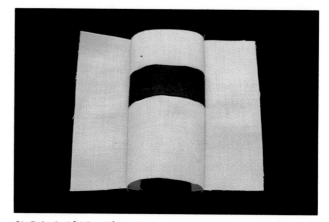

6) Stitch 1½" × 2½" (3.8 × 6.5 cm) rectangle of house fabric to the top of the window; stitch 2½" (6.5 cm) square to the bottom of the window. Stitch one 1½" × 4½" (3.8 × 11.5 cm) rectangle to each side of pieced window section.

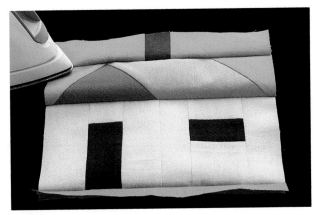

7) Stitch pieced door section and pieced window section together. Stitch pieced strips and ground strip together. Press quilt block.

8) Repeat steps 2 to 7 for remaining quilt blocks. Arrange blocks in rows of three.

9) Cut sashing strips with connecting squares (page 19) and attach to the quilt blocks; you will need 24 sashing pieces with a cut width of 2" (5 cm) and sixteen 2" (5 cm) connecting squares.

10) Cut and attach border strips (pages 20 to 25); cut width of border strips is 3½" (9 cm).

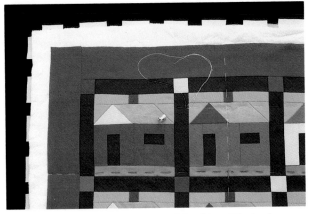

11) Cut 40" (102 cm) square of backing fabric. Layer and baste quilt top, batting, and backing (pages 26 and 27).

12) Quilt, using stitch-in-the-ditch method (pages 34 and 35) around blocks, sashing, and borders; quilt houses as desired. Cut and apply binding (page 37); cut width of binding is 2" (5 cm). For wall hanging, attach fabric sleeve (page 39). (Contrasting thread was used to show detail.)

More Houses Designs

Houses designs allow you to have fun experimenting with colors and textures. Select colors to suggest a mood or time of day. Or choose colors or fabrics to depict a particular type of house.

Bright crayon colors create a cheerful coverlet for a child's room. The twin-size bed quilt shown above consists of 48 quilt blocks, six blocks across and six down. The finished size of the quilt including a 3½" (9 cm) border, is about 65½" × 85½" (166.8 × 217.3 cm).

Houses quilt blocks can be embellished with appliqués, embroidery, or decorative buttons to add landscaping or architectural details.

Daytime effect is created by using sunny colors for the houses and black for the doors and windows.

Embellished houses are decorated with lace, trims, beads, and buttons for a whimsical effect.

Ocean Waves

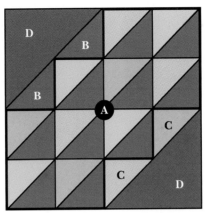

The Ocean Waves design is a traditional quilt design with rows of triangles that create a gentle flowing motion. Planning the color scheme for an Ocean Waves quilt can look difficult, but is actually simple to do.

The waves portion of an Ocean Waves block is made from ten triangle-squares plus four additional small triangles. Two large triangles in opposite corners complete the block. The grid-piecing method (page 44) is used to construct the triangle-squares. If you are unfamiliar with this type of construction, you may want to make the smaller Pine Trees project (page 43) before making the more challenging Ocean Waves project. The large triangles at the corners form the squares in the design when the blocks are stitched together.

For the quilt shown opposite, choose one dark-colored solid fabric, which will be used for one half of each triangle-square; repeating one fabric in each triangle-square gives the quilt a unified color scheme. Choose eight light-colored solid fabrics, which will be used for the remaining half of the triangle-squares. To minimize the appearance of the seams in the pieced squares, choose a printed fabric for the large triangles.

The instructions that follow are for a wall hanging or lap quilt made from twenty-four 8" (20.5 cm) quilt blocks. The finished quilt with a double lapped border measures about 40" × 56" (102 × 142 cm).

✂ Cutting Directions

For grid-pieced triangle-squares (**A**), cut eight 9½" × 15" (24.3 × 38 cm) rectangles from dark-colored solid fabric, and cut one 9½" × 15" (24.3 × 38 cm) rectangle from each of the eight light-colored solid fabrics.

Cut twenty-four 2⅞" (7.2 cm) squares from dark-colored solid fabric; cut squares in half diagonally to make 48 small triangles (**B**). Cut three 2⅞" (7.2 cm) squares from each of eight light-colored solid fabrics; cut squares in half diagonally to make 48 more small triangles (**C**). Cut twenty-four 4⅞" (12.2 cm) squares from printed fabric; cut squares in half diagonally to make 48 large triangles (**D**).

YOU WILL NEED

1⅛ **yd. (1.05 m) dark-colored solid fabric** for one half of each triangle-square.

⅓ **yd. (0.32 m) each of eight light-colored solid fabrics,** or eight fat quarters, for remaining halves of triangle-squares.

½ **yd. (0.5 m) printed fabric** for large triangles.

¼ **yd. (0.25 m) fabric** for 1" (2.5 cm) inner border.

⅔ **yd. (0.63 m) fabric** for 3" (7.5 cm) outer border.

½ **yd. (0.5 m) fabric** for binding.

2½ **yd. (2.3 m) fabric** for backing.

Batting, about 44" × 60" (112 × 152.5 cm).

How to Make an Ocean Waves Quilt

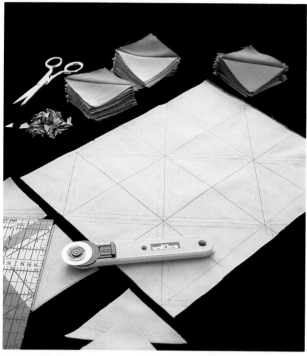

1) Assemble triangle-squares from 9½" × 15" (24.3 × 38 cm) rectangles, as on page 44, steps 1 to 4; in step 1, draw grids of 2⅞" (7.2 cm) squares, five across and three down. Make separate stacks of triangle-squares from each grid.

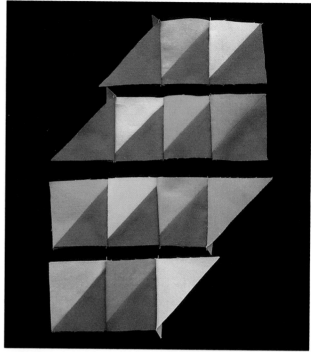

2) Stitch triangle-squares and small triangles into four rows as shown; use a triangle-square from each stack, using two of the colors twice. This will evenly distribute colors throughout the block.

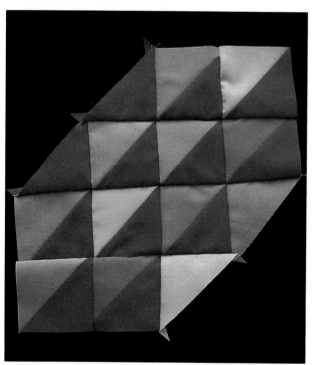

3) Stitch rows together as shown, finger-pressing seams in opposite directions. Do not press.

4) Stitch one large triangle to the diagonal edge of pieced section, taking care not to stretch bias edges. Repeat on opposite edge. Press block, pressing seam allowances toward large triangles. Trim points that extend beyond block.

5) Repeat steps 2 to 4 for the remaining blocks; in step 2, randomly select two colors to be used twice. Arrange blocks, six across and four down, making sure that dark-colored triangles are next to light-colored solid triangles.

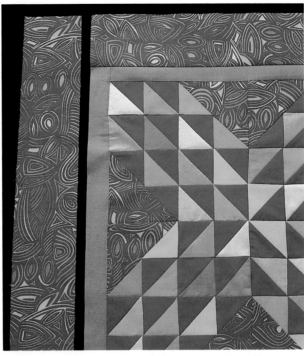

6) Stitch blocks into rows; stitch rows together, finger-pressing seam allowances in opposite directions. Press quilt top. Cut and attach border strips (pages 20 to 25); cut width of inner border strips is 1½" (3.8 cm) and cut width of outer border is 3½" (9 cm).

7) Cut backing about 4" (10 cm) larger than quilt top. Layer and baste quilt top, batting, and backing (pages 26 and 27). Quilt (pages 28 to 35).

8) Cut and apply binding (page 37); cut width of binding is 2½" (6.5 cm). For wall hanging, attach fabric sleeve (page 39).

More Ocean Waves Designs

The Ocean Waves design illustrates how different color combinations can be used to create different effects. For a subtle look, combine a light-colored solid fabric in each triangle-square with a softly contrasting solid. For a more random effect, use eight light-colored and eight sharply contrasting dark-colored fabrics for the grid-pieced triangle-squares.

Design squares that are formed between the quilt blocks can be made from various fabrics, as shown in this quilt. The triangle-squares consist of a single light color and eight dark colors.

Subtle color variation is achieved in this quilt by using hand-dyed fabrics. A soft pink is used in each triangle-square, and eight shades of pinks, blues, and lavenders are used for the contrasting fabrics. The printed fabric unifies the design, and stipple quilting (pages 34 and 35) adds texture throughout the quilt.

Vibrant pattern is created in this quilt by using scraps of eight light-colored and eight dark-colored fabrics for the triangle-squares.

Tumbling Blocks

The Tumbling Blocks quilt design, also called Building Blocks and Baby's Blocks, allows for optical effects that are simple to achieve through the use of fabrics in light, medium, and dark colors. The blocks are placed with the light sides facing in the same direction for a three-dimensional look.

Tumbling Blocks are constructed using 60° diamonds. They can be cut quickly using a tool such as an Easy-Six™, designed for 60° diamonds. This tool eliminates any calculations and has markings for several sizes.

Three diamonds are stitched together to form a block unit. The blocks are joined at the sides in rows, and the rows are then stitched together. This quilt design does not lend itself to chainstitching; the blocks must be accurately pieced, one seam at a time, making this a more challenging project. For this reason, the Tumbling Blocks quilt design is usually used for smaller projects, such as wall hangings and crib quilts.

Tumbling Blocks quilts can be made with as few as three fabrics in light, medium, and dark colors or with a different fabric for every diamond in the quilt.

The instructions that follow are for a quilt made from diamonds with a finished width of 2" (5 cm). The finished quilt with a double lapped border measures about 25" × 40" (63.5 × 102 cm), a size suitable for a wall hanging or crib quilt.

✂ Cutting Directions

Cut 60° diamonds (below) from fabrics in light (**A**), medium (**B**), and dark (**C**) colors; use the markings on the tool for a finished width of 2" (5 cm). You will need 66 light-colored diamonds, 55 medium-colored diamonds, and 55 dark-colored diamonds.

YOU WILL NEED

3/8 **yd. (0.35 m) fabric** each in light, medium, and dark colors; or scraps of fabrics in light, medium, and dark colors.
1/4 **yd. (0.25 m) fabric** for inner border.
1/2 **yd. (0.5 m) fabric** for outer border.
3/8 **yd. (0.35 m) fabric** for binding.
1 1/4 **yd. (1.15 m) fabric** for backing.
Batting, about 29" × 44" (73.5 × 112 cm).

How to Cut 60° Diamonds

1) Cut the diamonds, using a tool designed for 60° diamonds. Cut fabric strips, using the marking for the desired finished size; strips will not measure finished size. To cut printed fabric, the tool and the fabric must be right sides up.

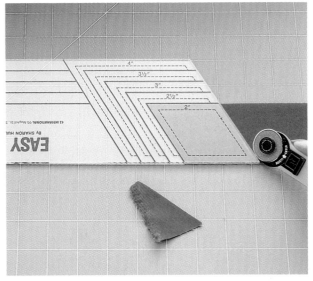

2) Trim selvage, using angled edge of tool. Rotate the tool, and place it at marking for desired finished size; cut along the angled edge of the ruler. Continue cutting additional diamonds from fabric strip.

How to Make a Tumbling Blocks Quilt

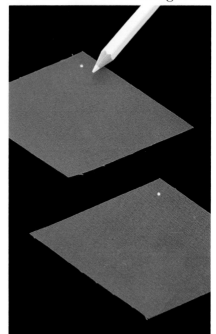

1) Mark wrong side of medium-colored diamonds where the ¼" (6 mm) seams will intersect, placing a dot at one wide-angle corner of each diamond.

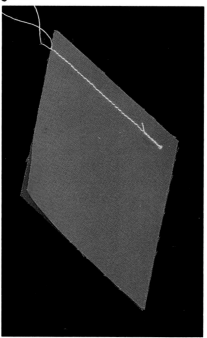

2) Align one medium-colored and one dark-colored diamond, right sides together, matching corners. Stitch from sharply pointed end exactly to the dot, with medium-colored diamond facing up; backstitch to secure ends of stitching.

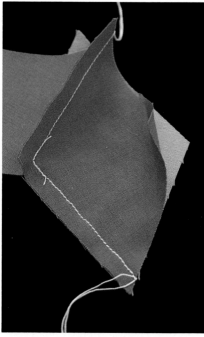

3) Align one side of a light-colored diamond to dark-colored diamond, right sides together, matching the edges and corners. Stitch from the pointed end exactly to the seam intersection, dark-colored diamond facing up; backstitch at ends.

4) Align light-colored diamond to medium-colored diamond, right sides together; stitch seam as in step 3, with light-colored diamond facing up. Press lightly, pressing seams toward darker fabric. Trim points that extend beyond block.

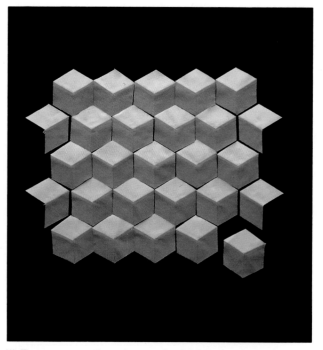

5) Repeat steps 1 to 4 to make 50 blocks. Arrange blocks into rows, with light-colored diamond at top of each block. Piece the remaining diamonds into partial blocks, as shown, to complete the quilt top, making sure to use diamonds of correct colors.

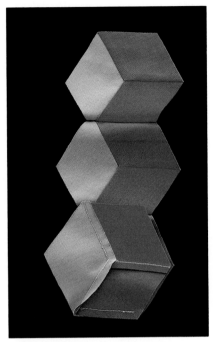

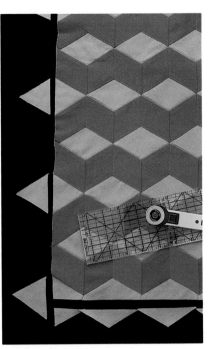

6) Join the blocks side-by-side, beginning and ending all seams ¼" (6 mm) from edges; do not catch seam allowances in stitching. Backstitch at ends.

7) Join the rows in zigzag manner, stitching each individual seam and making sure not to catch the seam allowances in stitching; backstitch at ends.

8) Piece remaining light-colored diamonds at lower edge, as shown. Press quilt top, pressing seams toward darker fabric. Trim outer edges even, using straightedge and rotary cutter; allow ¼" (6 mm) seam allowances.

9) Cut and attach border strips (pages 20 to 25); cut width is 1¼" (3.2 cm) for inner border and 3½" (9 cm) for outer border. Cut backing 4" (10 cm) larger than the quilt top. Layer and baste the quilt top, batting, and backing (pages 26 and 27).

10) Quilt, using stitch-in-the-ditch method (pages 34 and 35); quilting may be done in horizontal rows, defining blocks. Cut and apply binding (page 37); the cut width of the binding is 2½" (6.5 cm). For wall hanging, attach fabric sleeve (page 39).

More Tumbling Blocks Designs

The Tumbling Blocks design, with its dimensional quality, has many variations. Try turning some of the quilt blocks to create motion in the quilt design. Add subtle visual interest by using unexpected fabrics randomly.

Tumbling blocks can be built around six-pointed stars (pages 72 and 73). The stars and blocks are made individually, then arranged as desired before they are stitched together. The arrangement of the stars may be either symmetrical or random. You may want to experiment with different arrangements to create illusions, such as blocks suspended in space.

A design alternative is to stitch blocks into motifs, such as pyramids, and appliqué the motifs onto a quilt top, as on page 73. This is a faster way to incorporate Tumbling Blocks into larger quilts.

Three random stars, interspersed among the blocks, create an interesting visual effect. Scraps of solids, with an occasional print, are used to add variety.

Horizontal rows are emphasized in the quilt below by the use of color. Repetition adds unity to the quilt.

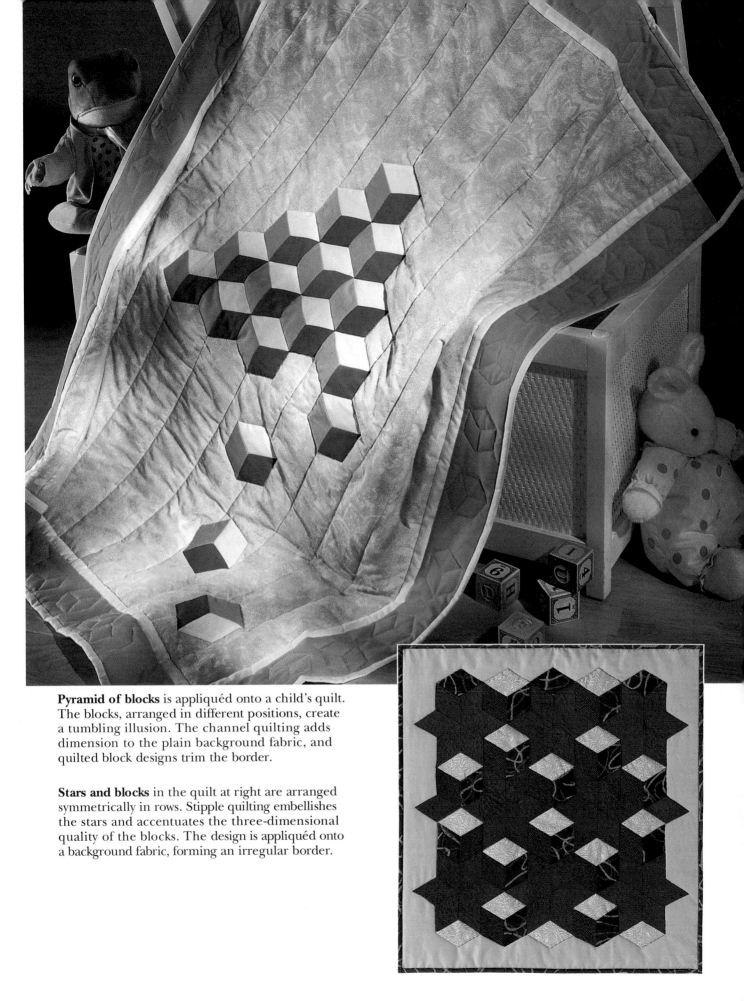

Pyramid of blocks is appliquéd onto a child's quilt. The blocks, arranged in different positions, create a tumbling illusion. The channel quilting adds dimension to the plain background fabric, and quilted block designs trim the border.

Stars and blocks in the quilt at right are arranged symmetrically in rows. Stipple quilting embellishes the stars and accentuates the three-dimensional quality of the blocks. The design is appliquéd onto a background fabric, forming an irregular border.

How to Make a Six-pointed Star

1) Cut diamonds the same size as the diamonds used for Tumbling Blocks (page 67), cutting six for each star. Mark diamonds where ¼" (6 mm) seams will intersect, placing a dot at each wide-angle corner.

2) Align two diamonds, right sides together, matching points. Stitch from one sharply pointed end exactly to dot; backstitch to secure ends of stitching.

3) Align a third diamond, matching raw edges and corners. Stitch from the dot to previous stitching; backstitch at ends.

4) Repeat steps 2 and 3, using the three remaining diamonds. Press seam allowances of each 3-diamond unit in same direction.

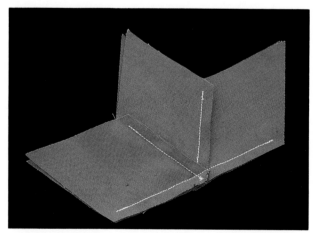

5) Place two 3-diamond units right sides together; pin, matching the seams at center. Stitch seam, beginning and ending ¼" (6 mm) from raw edge; backstitch at ends. Trim points that extend beyond edge.

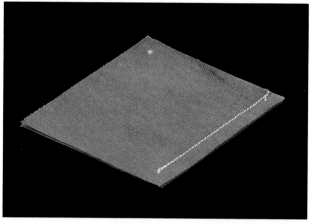

6) Press from wrong side, working from center out, and pressing seam allowances in one direction.

How to Make a Tumbling Blocks Quilt with Six-pointed Stars

1) Make desired number of stars, opposite. Make desired number of Tumbling Blocks as on page 68, steps 1 to 4. Arrange blocks and stars as desired.

2) Add individual diamonds as necessary to fill in design around stars. Make and add partial blocks as on page 68, step 5.

3) Stitch units together, stitching each individual seam and backstitching at ends of seams. Whenever possible, stitch units together in rows, adding extra diamonds and stars as rows are joined.

4) Complete quilt as on page 69, steps 8 to 10; quilt around stars, then along blocks.

How to Apply a Tumbling Blocks Appliqué

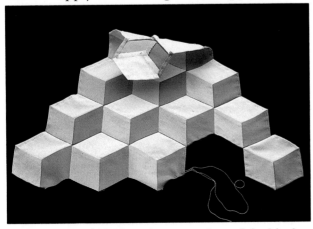

1) Turn under ¼" (6 mm) at raw edges of the block motif; baste, then press in place.

2) Position design on quilt top as desired; pin or baste in place. Secure pressed edges as on page 78, step 4.

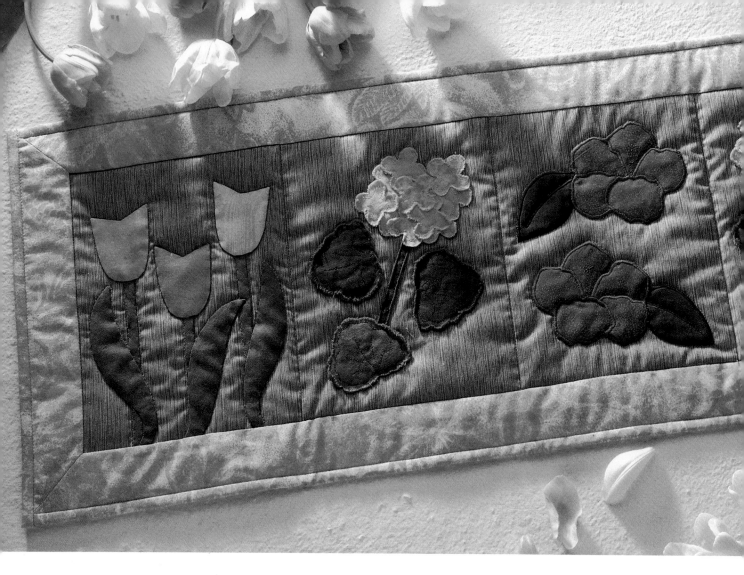

Appliquéd Quilts

Three different methods of machine appliqué are popular for appliquéd quilts: blindstitched, frayed, and satin-stitched. Each method has a different look and can be used to match the style of the quilt, from traditional to contemporary.

Blindstitched appliqué has the look of traditional hand stitching, but uses a faster machine technique. The appliqué is stitched to the quilt block using monofilament nylon thread for the needle thread and the machine blindstitch. The appliqués are made by shaping the fabric around cardboard templates. The templates do not include seam allowances; estimated ¼" (6 mm) seam allowances are added when the fabric is cut. Bias tape may be used for flower stems or wherever a narrow strip is needed, eliminating the need for a template.

Frayed appliqué has exposed raw edges. To secure the appliqué, the stitching is done inside the edges of the design. For a frayed appearance, the appliqué is then brushed with a stiff brush, or, provided the fabrics have been prewashed, a more natural frayed look can be achieved by laundering. Frayed appliqué

gives added texture and interest to a quilt and has a more contemporary look.

Satin-stitched appliqué has machine satin stitching that secures the appliqué and covers the raw edges of the fabric, for a more defined appearance. Use this method for easier application of intricately shaped pieces or appliqués cut from printed fabric. Satin-stitch appliqué is durable and is therefore a good choice for quilts that will be laundered frequently.

When stitching appliqués, decrease the needle thread tension and use a bobbin thread that matches the quilt top. To prevent the appliqués from puckering, apply a piece of tear-away stabilizer to the wrong side of the quilt top.

The instructions that follow are for the Garden Row Appliqué Sampler, above. This project incorporates all three methods of appliqué and may be used as a table runner or wall hanging. The sampler is made from five quilt blocks, each measuring 6½" × 8½" (16.3 × 21.8 cm). The finished project measures about 35½" × 11½" (90.3 × 29.3 cm).

Types of Appliqués

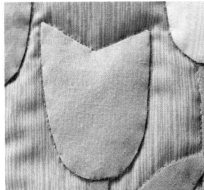

Blindstitched appliqué resembles traditional hand stitching but is sewn with the machine blindstitch.

Frayed appliqué is a contemporary style with exposed raw edges.

Satin-stitched appliqué, sewn with machine satin stitching, has more defined edges.

✂ Cutting Directions

Cut five 7" × 9" (18 × 23 cm) rectangles from fabric background.

For tulips on two quilt blocks, use the patterns on page 76 to make cardboard templates for the tulip flower and tulip leaf. Cut six flowers and six leaves from fabric as on page 78, step 1; turn the template over to cut two of the leaves. Cut six stems from bias tape to desired lengths. Three leaves, three flowers, and three stems are used for each quilt block.

For geraniums on two quilt blocks, cut six leaves and 16 to 20 florets, using the patterns on page 76. Cut two fabric stems ¼" × 3" (6 mm × 7.5 cm). Three leaves, eight to ten florets, and one stem are used for each quilt block.

For hibiscus on one quilt block, cut two flowers and two leaves, using the patterns on page 76; turn the pattern over to cut one of the leaves.

YOU WILL NEED

⅜ yd. (0.35 m) fabric for background.

¾ yd. (0.7 m) fabric for 1½" (3.8 cm) border, backing, and binding.

Fabric scraps for flowers and leaves; double-fold bias tape for tulip stems.

Batting, about 13" × 35" (33 × 89 cm).

Cardboard, spray starch, and monofilament nylon thread for blindstitched appliqués.

¾ yd. (0.7 m) tear-away stabilizer.

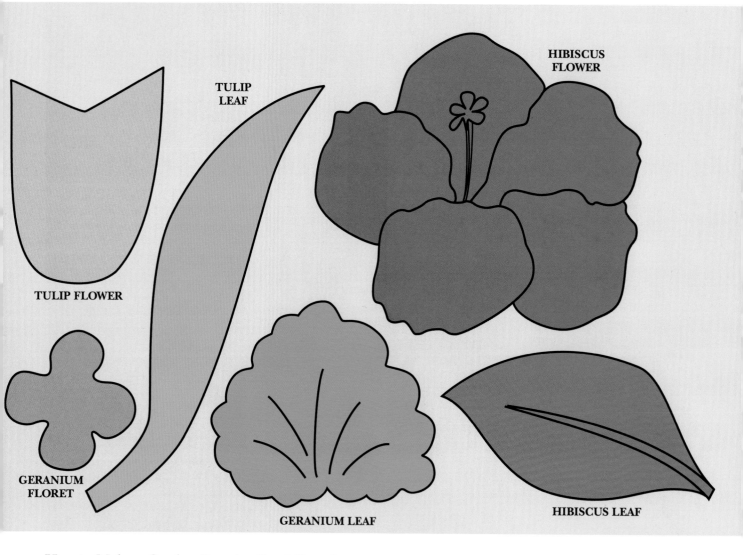

TULIP FLOWER

TULIP LEAF

HIBISCUS FLOWER

GERANIUM FLORET

GERANIUM LEAF

HIBISCUS LEAF

How to Make a Garden Row Appliqué Sampler

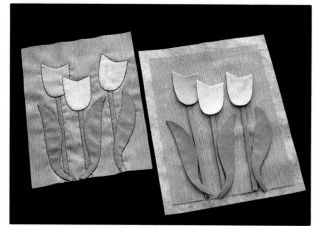

1) **Follow** steps 2 to 5 on page 78 for the blindstitched appliqués, arranging pieces for three tulips on quilt block as shown; place bottom of leaves at raw edge of block. For stems, trim away one folded edge of bias tape to reduce bulk. Repeat for second quilt block.

2) **Follow** steps 1 to 7 on page 79 for the frayed appliqués, arranging pieces for one geranium on quilt block as shown. Repeat for second quilt block.

3) Follow steps 1 to 4 on page 80 for the satin-stitched appliqués, arranging pieces for two hibiscus flowers on quilt block as shown.

4) Stitch stamens on hibiscus, using free-motion sewing (pages 34 and 35).

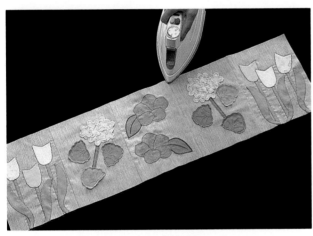

5) Stitch blocks together in ¼" (6 mm) seams, as shown. Press the quilt top, taking care not to overpress appliqués.

6) Cut and attach border strips (pages 20 to 25); cut width of border strips is 2" (5 cm). Cut backing 13" × 35" (33 × 89 cm); layer and baste the quilt top, batting, and backing (pages 26 and 27).

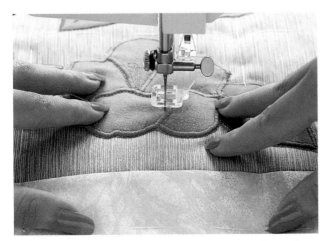

7) Quilt, using stitch-in-the-ditch method, along the seamlines (pages 34 and 35). Quilt around flowers. If desired, quilt along design lines of hibiscus, to define petals. (Contrasting thread was used to show detail.)

8) Cut and apply binding (page 37); cut width of binding is 2" (5 cm). For wall hanging, attach fabric sleeve (page 39).

How to Sew a Blindstitched Appliqué

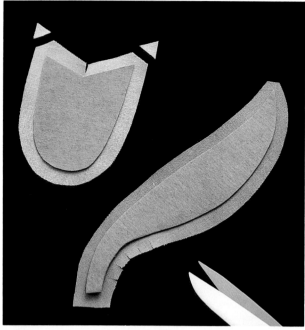

1) Cut cardboard templates to the *finished size* of appliqué pieces. Place template on fabric. Adding ¼" (6 mm) seam allowances, cut around template, using rotary cutter. Clip inside curves and corners almost to template; trim outside corners.

2) Spray starch in small bowl; dab starch on section of seam allowance. With tip of dry iron, press seam allowance over edge of template; press until spray starch dries. Continue pressing around the appliqué. Remove the template, and press appliqué, right side up.

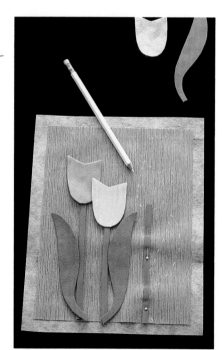

3) Position appliqué design on the quilt block; mark the placement of the pieces, using chalk. Position tear-away stabilizer, cut larger than design, on wrong side of fabric. Pin or baste pieces in place; for layered design, apply first layer only.

4) Set machine for short blindstitch, with the stitch width about ¹⁄₁₆" (1.5 mm); use monofilament nylon thread in the needle. Blindstitch around pieces, catching edge with widest swing of stitch. (Contrasting thread was used to show detail.)

5) Pin or baste the second layer in place, and blindstitch. Repeat as necessary for any remaining layers. Remove tear-away stabilizer, taking care not to distort stitches.

How to Sew a Frayed Appliqué

1) Cut the appliqué pieces, using patterns; do not add seam allowances. Mark any design lines.

2) Position the appliqué design on quilt block; mark the placement of pieces, using chalk.

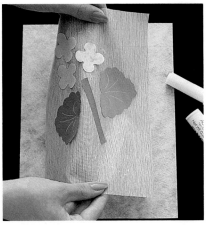

3) Glue-baste pieces in place ¼" (6 mm) from edges; for layered design, apply first layer only. Place tear-away stabilizer on wrong side of fabric.

4) Stitch around pieces, stitching ⅛" (3 mm) from raw edge; some designs may require free-motion sewing (pages 34 and 35).

5) Glue-baste the second layer in place; stitch as in step 4. Repeat as necessary for any remaining layers.

6) Stitch on any design lines, using free-motion sewing, if necessary. Remove tear-away stabilizer, taking care not to distort stitches.

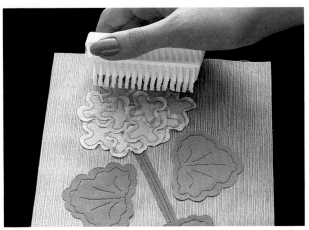

7) Brush edges of appliqué, if desired, using a stiff brush; this will ravel edges to add more texture.

How to Sew a Satin-stitched Appliqué

1) Cut appliqué pieces, using patterns; do not add seam allowances. Mark any design lines; patterns may be cut apart to serve as guide for marking.

2) Position pieces on quilt block; mark placement, using chalk. Position tear-away stabilizer on wrong side of fabric. Glue-baste or pin pieces in place; for layered design, apply first layer only.

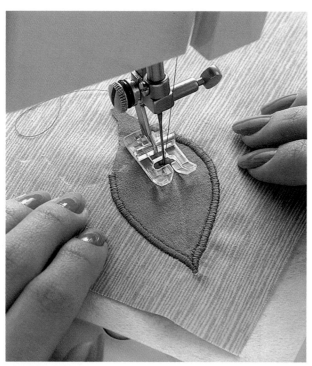

3) Set machine for short, wide zigzag stitch; use machine embroidery thread in needle. Satin stitch around pieces; do not satin stitch edges that will be overlapped by other pieces. Add details, such as veins of leaves; for veins, use narrow zigzag stitch and taper ends.

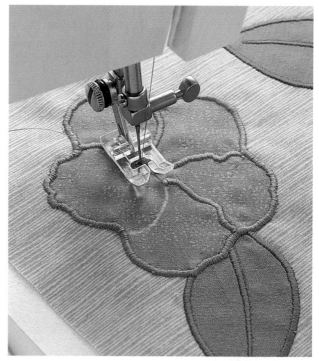

4) Glue-baste second layer in place; satin stitch as in step 3. Repeat for any remaining layers. Remove the tear-away stabilizer, taking care not to distort stitches.

Satin-stitching Techniques for Appliqués

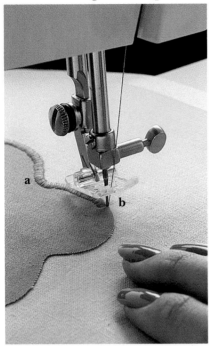

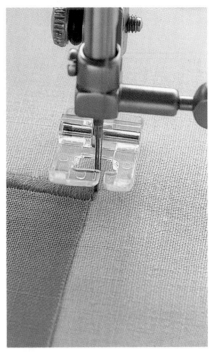

Curves. Pivot the fabric frequently, pivoting with the needle down. For inside curves, pivot with needle at inner edge of stitching (**a**); for outside curves, pivot with needle on outer edge of stitching (**b**).

Inside corners. Stitch past corner a distance equal to width of stitch, stopping with the needle down at the inner edge of stitching. Pivot fabric, and satin stitch next side of appliqué.

Outside corners. Stitch one stitch past edge of appliqué, stopping with needle down at outer edge of stitching. Pivot fabric, and satin stitch next side of appliqué.

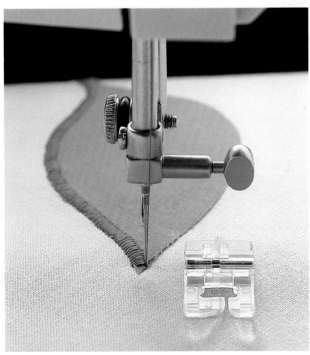

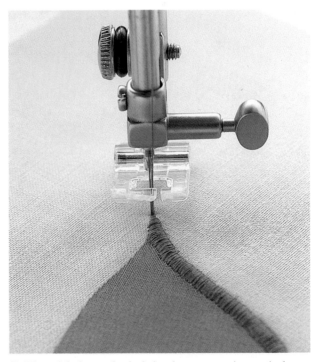

Points. 1) Stitch, stopping when inner edge of satin stitching meets the opposite side of the appliqué. Pivot the fabric slightly; continue stitching, gradually narrowing stitch width to 0 and stopping at point. (Presser foot was removed to show detail.)

2) Pivot fabric, and stitch back over previous stitches, gradually widening the stitch width to original width. Pivot fabric slightly, and stitch next side of appliqué.

More Appliqué Designs

The appliqué methods used for the Garden Row Appliqué Sampler can be used for many designs. Use the appliqué patterns available at quilt stores, or design your own appliqués, using books, cards, and artwork for design ideas.

Frayed appliqué and authentic African prints were used for the quilt above. Primitive figures were made from two fabric layers, the top layer cut smaller than the first.

Blindstitched appliqué is used for the quilt at left. The easy-to-cut pieces are blindstitched in place.

Satin-stitched appliqué (opposite) is used for the fish, which were cut from a printed fabric. A string-pieced quilt top (page 95) provides the background; some strips were pieced together before they were applied to the foundation.

Crazy Quilts

Crazy quilting allows you to use scraps of all kinds to make quilts in an unplanned, nonprecise pattern. Crazy quilting was popular during the Victorian era, when scraps of silk were used to complement the lavish decorating style. Patches were basted on a foundation fabric and secured with hand embroidery stitches.

Today, machine embroidery makes these quilts faster to sew. Experiment with decorative threads, such as metallics and rayons, for embroidery stitches. Mix a variety of fabrics, such as satins, lamés, denims, and bits of old table or bed linens.

Crazy quilts can be sewn using either the traditional method or the stitch-and-flip method. For the traditional method, the patches are basted to a foundation fabric with the edges turned under, then secured with decorative stitches, such as feather and herringbone stitches. Or for faster construction, the patches can be arranged with the raw edges exposed; decorative satin stitches secure the patches and finish the edges. For the stitch-and-flip method, the patches are secured without decorative stitching. This method works well for quilts with a contemporary look.

Use a lightweight fabric, such as muslin, for the foundation, in a light color that will not show through the fabrics in the quilt top. The foundation fabric is usually cut into blocks, and the completed blocks sewn together to make the quilt top. For small quilts, the patches can be applied to one large foundation.

Traditionally, batting was not used with crazy quilts. To secure the quilt top to the backing, the quilts were tacked at the seamlines. If batting is used, the blocks should be tacked or quilted at frequent intervals to keep the batting from shifting.

Irregular patches of fabric are randomly stitched onto a square of foundation fabric, and the edges are trimmed to make a crazy-quilt block.

Tips for Making a Crazy Quilt

Use machine embroidery thread for smooth, even decorative stitching with sheen.

Control slippery fabrics, such as some silks, by fusing them to lightweight interfacing.

Use woven lamé for a decorative effect. Preshrink the lamé with a steam iron, and fuse it to knitted interfacing for strength and to prevent raveling.

Use a larger needle and loosen the needle thread tension when stitching with metallic thread. Check to see that the needle does not have burrs.

YOU WILL NEED

Fabric scraps for quilt blocks.

Lightweight muslin for foundation fabric.

Fabric for borders, if desired, yardage determined as on page 20.

Fabric for backing, yardage determined as on page 26.

Fabric for binding, yardage determined as on page 36.

Batting, if desired, about 4" (10 cm) larger than quilt.

Machine embroidery thread for a crazy quilt made by traditional method.

How to Make a Crazy Quilt Using the Traditional Method

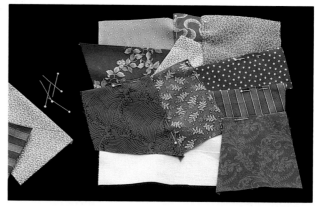

1) Cut foundation slightly larger than finished block size plus ½" (1.3 cm) for seam allowances. Cut a patch for one corner; pin in place. Cut another patch to overlap first patch; turn under ¼" (6 mm) on edge that will overlap. Pin or baste in place.

2) Continue to attach patches until foundation is covered. Turn under ¼" (6 mm) on all edges except those on outside of block; pin or baste in place.

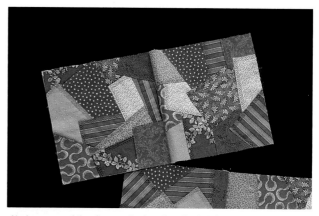

3) Stitch along pressed edges, using decorative stitches, working from center to edges; pull needle thread to underside, and knot. Trim the block to the finished size plus ½" (1.3 cm) for seam allowances.

4) Arrange blocks as desired; stitch blocks together into rows. Stitch rows together, finger-pressing seam allowances in opposite directions. Press quilt top. Cut and attach border strips (pages 20 to 25).

5) Cut backing (page 26). If batting is desired, cut batting 4" (10 cm) larger than quilt top. Layer and baste quilt top, batting, and backing (pages 26 and 27). Machine-tack or quilt (pages 28 to 35) at frequent intervals. Cut and apply binding (page 37).

Alternate method. Follow steps 1 and 2, except overlap patches and do not turn under edges. Stitch over raw edges, using wide decorative stitches; work from center to edges. Trim block to finished size plus ½" (1.3 cm) for seam allowances. Complete quilt as in steps 4 and 5.

How to Make a Crazy Quilt Using the Stitch-and-Flip Method

1) Cut foundation fabric slightly larger than finished block size plus ½" (1.3 cm) for seam allowances. Cut a patch, and place in center or corner of foundation; pin in place. Place a second patch on first patch, right sides together, aligning one edge. Stitch ¼" (6 mm) seam along aligned edges.

2) Flip the second patch right side up; press. Pin in place. Continue to attach patches until foundation is covered; press under ¼" (6 mm) seam allowance on edges that will not be covered.

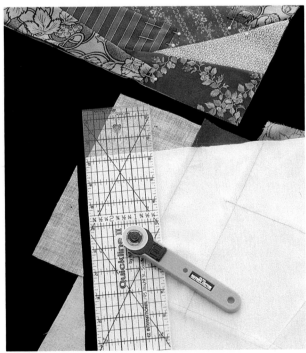

3) Trim blocks to finished size plus ½" (1.3 cm) for seam allowances. Pin any unstitched folded edges to foundation.

4) Secure unstitched folded edges as for blindstitched appliqué on page 78, step 4. Finish quilt as in steps 4 and 5, opposite. For wall hanging, attach fabric sleeve (page 39). (Contrasting thread was used to show detail.)

More Crazy-quilt Designs

Crazy-quilt variations are limitless. Experiment with any idea, because there are no rules for crazy quilting. For a contemporary look, slash the quilt top and insert a contrasting strip of fabric.

To save time when making a large quilt top, you can alternate patched blocks with plain blocks. Quilt the plain blocks, using a decorative template, to add a new dimension to the quilt.

Contrasting lamé strips have been inserted to give this crazy quilt a contemporary look, and metallic threads were used to carry out the effect. The quilt was made using the traditional method.

How to Add Contrasting Strips to a Crazy-quilt Top

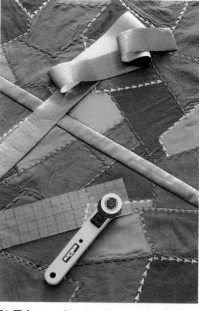

1) Cut insert strip desired finished width plus ½" (1.3 cm). Slash quilt top at desired angle. Subtract ¼" (6 mm) seam allowance from one-half the finished width of insert strip; trim from each slashed edge.

2) Apply interfacing to lamé. Pin and stitch one slashed edge to strip in ¼" (6 mm) seam, with right sides together and insert strip facing up; extend strip beyond ends of block. Press strip right side up.

3) Trim ends of strip even with block. Stitch remaining section of block to opposite side of insert strip, with strip facing up. Repeat steps for additional strips, if desired.

Crazy-quilt blocks and plain blocks have been alternated in this quilt. The plain blocks were quilted using a decorative template. This quilt was made using the stitch-and-flip method.

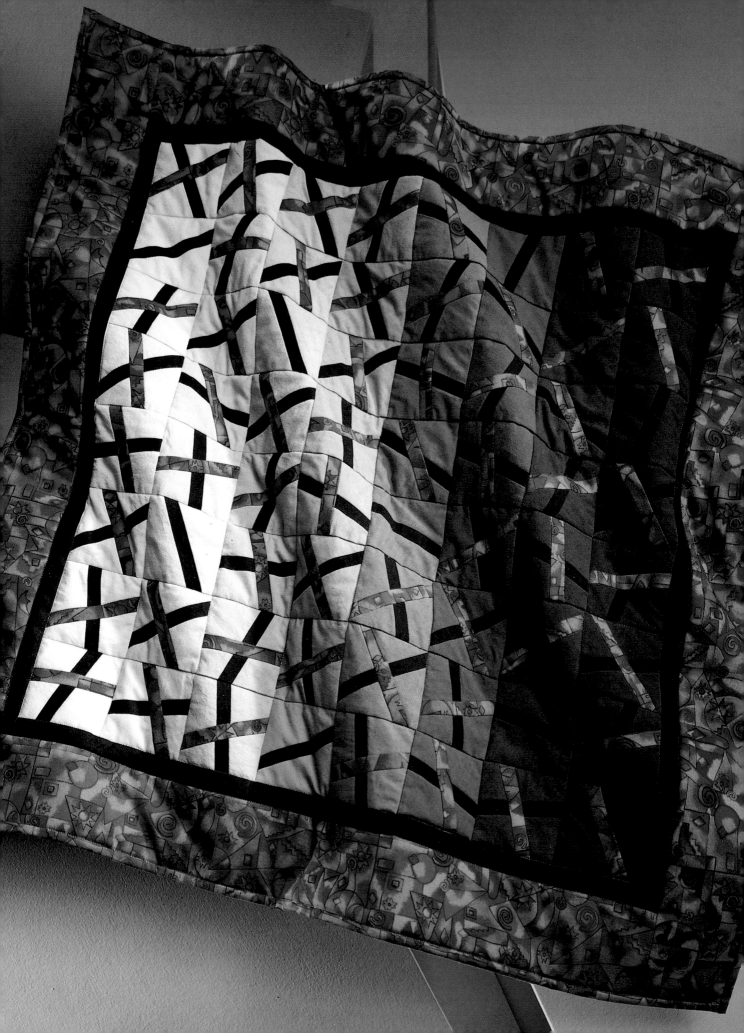

Contemporary Crazy Quilts

This contemporary variation of crazy quilting looks intricate, but is actually quick and easy to piece. For a gradation of colors in the rows of the quilt blocks, hand-dyed fabrics (page 10) work well for the background fabrics. Solid-colored and printed fabric strips that match the border fabrics are used for contrasting strips in the blocks.

The instructions that follow are for a wall hanging made from sixty-four 3" (7.5 cm) quilt blocks. The finished quilt with a double lapped border measures about 32" (81.5 cm) square.

✂ Cutting Directions

Cut four 2¼" × 18" (6 × 46 cm) strips (page 12) from each hand-dyed fabric. Cut eight 1" (2.5 cm) crosswise strips from the fabric for the inner border; cut strips at the center foldline of the fabric to make 16 strips. Cut eight 1" (2.5 cm) strips from the fabric for the outer border. Cut one 3½" (9 cm) square template from heavy cardboard or plastic.

YOU WILL NEED

One hand-dyed fabric packet of eight fat quarters.

⅔ **yd. (0.63 m) solid-colored fabric** to be used for ¾" (2 cm) inner border and contrasting insert strip.

1 yd. (0.95 m) printed fabric to be used for 3" (7.5 cm) outer border and for contrasting insert strip.

1 yd. (0.95 m) fabric for backing.

Batting, about 36" (91.5 cm) square.

Heavy cardboard or plastic for template.

How to Make a Contemporary Crazy Quilt

1) Stitch two hand-dyed strips of the same color to each side of 1" (2.5 cm) strip from inner border fabric, right sides together. Repeat for remaining 15 strips. Press seam allowances toward center strip.

2) Cut four squares from each pieced strip, using template and rotary cutter; vary the angle of the strip on each square. Strips may be cut with three or four layers stacked together.

3) Set aside eight squares, one of each fabric color.

(Continued on next page)

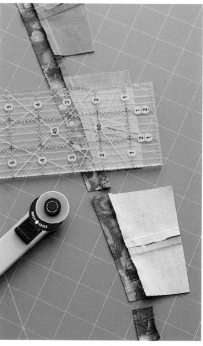

4) Slash an angled cut through each remaining square, using straightedge; cut across insert strip and vary angle. Arrange corresponding portions in order, separating them in two stacks. Squares will be rejoined in step 7.

5) Stitch slashed edge of one portion from each square to edge of 1" (2.5 cm) strip from outer border fabric, right sides together; chainstitch portions together, extending the strip ½" (1.3 cm) beyond edges.

6) Press seam allowances toward strip. Trim ends of strip even with edges of squares, using straightedge or template as a guide.

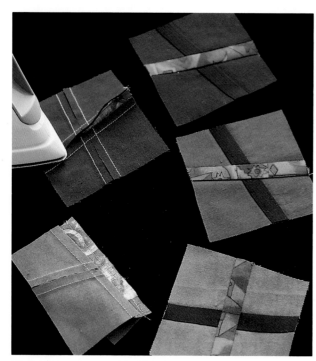

7) Stitch corresponding portions of squares to the opposite edge of strips to make blocks. Press seam allowances toward center of strip, taking care not to stretch bias edges.

8) Arrange blocks into vertical rows of each color, turning contrasting strips in different directions; include blocks set aside in step 3, placing them in random positions within each row.

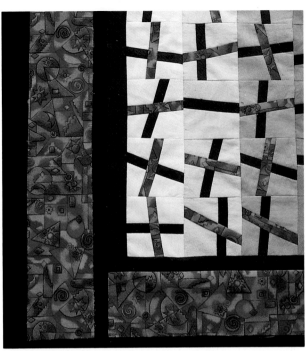

9) Stitch blocks of each color into rows; stitch rows together, finger-pressing seam allowances in opposite directions. Press quilt top.

10) Cut and attach border strips (pages 20 to 25); cut width of inner border strips is 1¼" (3.2 cm), and cut width of outer border strips is 3½" (9 cm).

11) Cut 36" (91.5 cm) square of backing fabric. Layer and baste quilt top, batting, and backing (pages 26 and 27).

12) Quilt around blocks and borders, using stitch-in-the-ditch method (pages 34 and 35). Cut and apply binding (page 37); cut width of binding is 2" (5 cm). For wall hanging, attach fabric sleeve (page 39).

String-pieced Quilts

String piecing is an easy way to create interesting and lively fabric arrangements. Traditionally used to make utility quilts, string piecing also lends itself to many contemporary designs.

String piecing is done on a foundation of fabric or paper. Strips of fabric in various widths are stitched to the foundation, and the completed blocks can be arranged for a variety of effects.

Lightweight muslin works well for the foundation. When string-piecing heavyweight fabrics, such as decorator fabrics, use a paper foundation to reduce bulk; the paper is removed from the completed block. Unprinted newsprint, available in large tablets, may be used as a foundation and is easy to remove.

Basic instructions are given on page 96 for making string-pieced quilt blocks of any size or shape. This technique is used for making all styles of string-pieced quilts, including those shown on page 99.

The color-gradated quilt shown opposite is a quick project made by string piecing. The gradation is easily achieved by the arrangement of light, medium, and dark quilt blocks. Hand-dyed fabrics work especially well for this project.

The instructions on pages 97 and 98 are for a color-gradated quilt made from thirty-two 8" (20.5 cm) quilt blocks. The finished quilt measures about 40" × 71" (102 × 180.5 cm), making it suitable for a wall hanging or lap quilt.

✄ Cutting Directions

For the color-gradated quilt, cut muslin foundation fabric into thirty-two 9" (23 cm) squares; this is the finished block size plus 1" (2.5 cm). Cut fabrics of light, medium, and dark colors into strips about 3" to 4" (7.5 to 10 cm) wide.

YOU WILL NEED

1¾ yd. (1.6 m) lightweight muslin for foundation fabric.

¼ yd. (0.25 m) fabric in each of five light, five medium, and five dark colors that blend, for a color-gradated quilt.

⅞ yd. (0.8 m) fabric for 4" (10 cm) border.

2¼ yd. (2.1 m) fabric for backing.

⅔ yd. (0.63 m) fabric for binding.

Batting, about 44" x 75" (112 × 190.5 cm).

Strips of fabric are stitched onto a square or rectangle of foundation fabric or paper, and the edges are trimmed to make a string-pieced quilt block. The strips may be placed horizontally, vertically, or diagonally.

How to Make a String-pieced Quilt Block

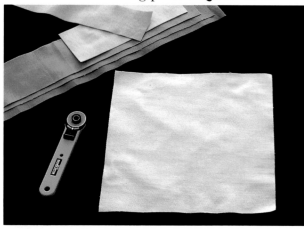

1) Cut a muslin or paper foundation 1" (2.5 cm) larger than finished block size. Cut strips of fabric, varying the width as desired; the cut length should extend beyond the edges of the foundation.

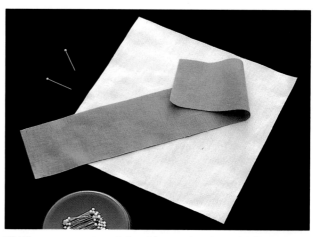

2) Place one strip, right side up, in the middle area of the foundation at desired angle; ends of strip should extend beyond edges of foundation. Pin in place.

3) Place second strip, right side down, along one long edge of first strip; pin. Stitch ¼" (6 mm) from aligned raw edges.

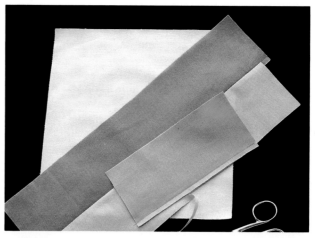

4) Fold strip right side up; press. Continue adding strips until half of foundation is covered. If desired, change angle of some strips, and stitch ¼" (6 mm) from raw edge of top strip; trim edges of strips even.

5) Repeat steps 3 and 4 for the opposite side of the foundation.

6) Trim block to finished size plus ½" (1.3 cm) for seam allowances. Remove paper foundation, if used.

How to Make a String-pieced Quilt with Color Gradations

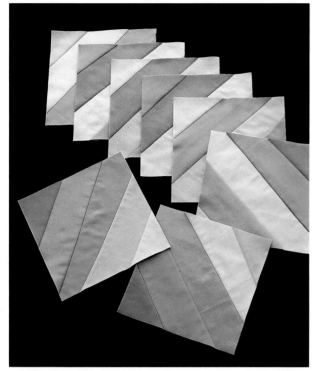

1) Separate the fabric strips into light, medium, and dark colors. Make eight string-pieced blocks (opposite), using light colors and setting strips on the diagonal; trim blocks to 8½" (21.8 cm) squares. These will be first and second rows of quilt.

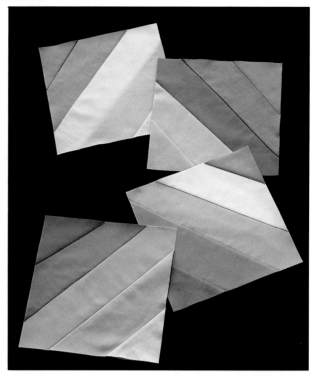

2) Make four blocks, using some light and some medium fabrics in each block, for third row.

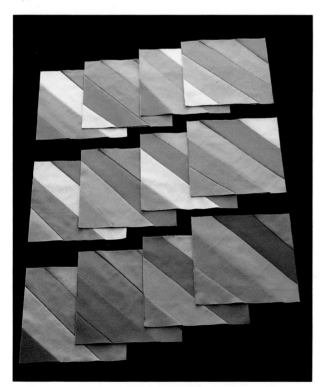

3) Make eight blocks, using medium colors; these will be fourth and fifth rows. Make four blocks, using some medium and some dark fabrics, for sixth row.

4) Make eight blocks, using dark colors; these will be seventh and eighth rows. Arrange blocks in all rows so strips form a zigzag pattern, as shown.

(Continued on next page)

5) Stitch each row of four blocks together. Stitch rows together, finger-pressing seams in opposite directions. Press quilt top.

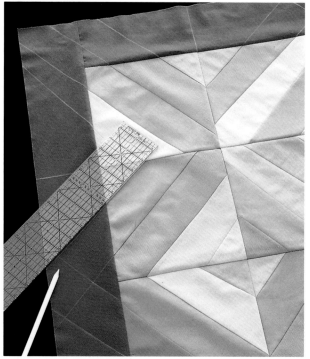

6) Cut and attach border strips (pages 20 to 25); the cut width of border strips is 4½" (11.5 cm). Using a straightedge, mark borders for quilting by randomly extending lines into the border.

7) Cut backing about 4" (10 cm) larger than quilt top; press. Layer and baste quilt top, batting, and backing (pages 26 and 27). Quilt on all seamlines, using stitch-in-the-ditch method (pages 34 and 35); extend stitching into border on marked lines.

8) Cut and apply binding (page 37); cut width of binding is 2½" (6.5 cm). For wall hanging, attach fabric sleeve (page 39).

More String-pieced Designs

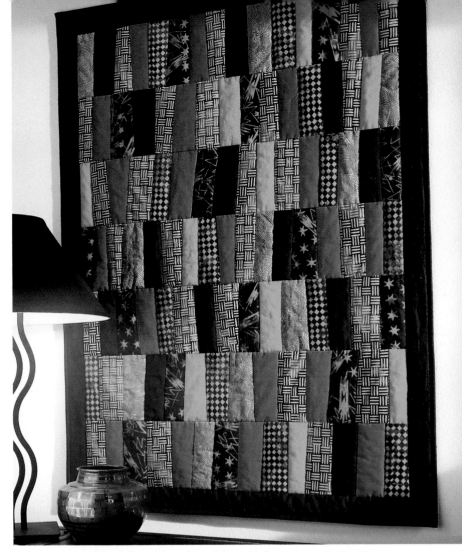

Vary the width and angle of the fabric strips for different effects. For a contemporary look, use bold colors or mix in specialty fabrics for drama. Experiment with different fabrics, block sizes, and block arrangements.

Decorator fabrics, cut in wide strips, make a quick and easy bed quilt. The full-size coverlet shown below consists of thirty-six 12" (30.5 cm) quilt blocks, six across and six down. The finished size of the quilt, including a 4" (10 cm) border, is about 80" (203.5 cm) square.

Contemporary look is achieved in this quilt by string-piecing long foundation strips instead of blocks.

Landscape Quilts

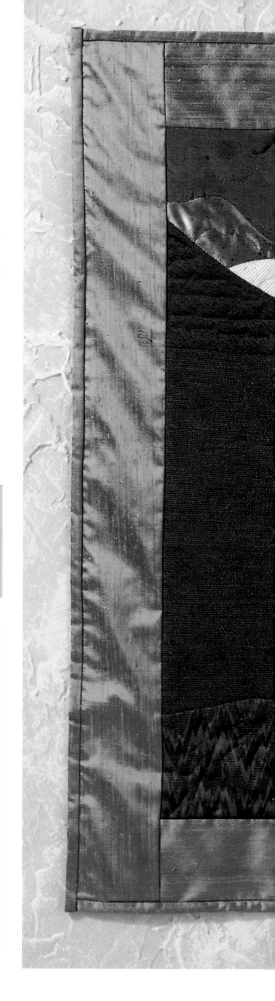

Strips of fabric can be used to portray landscapes, which are designed over a piece of foundation fabric. The strips are cut freehand, and the scene is created in layers, usually working from the top to the bottom. The exposed edges of the strips are turned under and secured with blindstitching. When designing landscapes, stand back and look at the project as you add the layered strips.

You may want to select fabrics that simulate the various textures of landscapes. Mottled prints, silk noils, and velveteens can be used to add depth to simple designs. For a country style, look for small calico prints to suggest texture.

Design inspiration can come from many sources. Photographs or paintings of landscapes can be adapted for landscape quilts. Before starting the project, you may want to make a sketch or actual-size drawing of the quilt.

YOU WILL NEED

Muslin for foundation fabric.
Scraps of fabric in choice of landscape colors.
Fabric for border, yardage determined as on page 20.
Fabric for backing, yardage determined as on page 26.
Fabric for binding, yardage determined as on page 36.
Batting, about 4" (10 cm) larger than quilt top.

Photographs are a good source of inspiration for landscape designs.

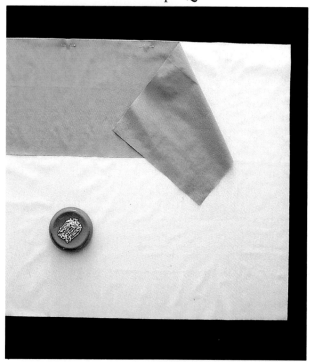

1) Cut foundation fabric slightly larger than finished landscape. Cut a fabric strip for the sky to the width of the foundation; pin to top of foundation.

2) Cut the fabric strip for the next layer, the width of foundation, curving upper edge as desired. Pin strip to the foundation, covering lower edge of sky and folding under scant ¼" (6 mm) along upper edge; clip curves as necessary.

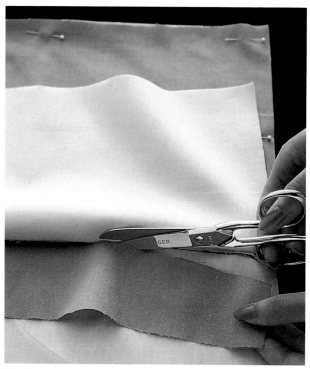

3) View pieces from a distance, with project on wall; adjust placement as desired. Trim excess fabric from previous layer.

4) Continue adding strips as in steps 2 and 3, until entire foundation is covered; some strips may be cut shorter to create hills or other landscaping details.

5) Cut additional shapes, such as clouds, and tuck behind a previous layer, if desired. Fold under exposed edges, or follow steps 1 and 2 on page 78 for blindstiched appliqué.

6) Blindstitch along pressed edges of strips, using monofilament nylon thread, as on page 78, step 4, folding back other layers as necessary. (Contrasting thread was used to show detail.)

7) Trim stitched landscape to finished size. Cut and attach border strips (pages 20 to 25). Cut backing and batting 4" (10 cm) larger than quilt top. Layer quilt top, batting, and backing (pages 26 and 27).

8) Quilt (pages 28 to 35); use stitch-in-the-ditch method along landscape strips and free-motion quilting for details. Cut and apply binding (page 37). For wall hanging, attach fabric sleeve (page 39).

More Landscape Designs

To add details to a landscape quilt, incorporate appliqués into the quilt design. Quilting lines also add detailing.

Pueblo (left) is made of Tumbling Blocks (page 67), applied as on page 73. The doors, windows, and ladders are satin-stitched as on pages 80 and 81.

Sunrise (below) was applied starting with the yellow center and working toward the sides. The green section was applied next, then the colorful fields. The pine trees are appliquéd, using the frayed method (page 79).

Folk-art quilt (right) is created using textured fabrics. The farm structures, appliquéd using the blindstitched method (page 78), are intentionally "crooked" for a rustic, country look.

Sunset (below, right) is the starting point of this quilt. Then the cliffs and stream are applied, using the same landscaping method. The quilting lines create the sun's rays, add a rugged quality to the cliffs, and suggest movement of the water.

Creative Sashing & Borders

Frame Sashing

Frame sashing is pieced to form a unique design of parallelograms and triangles. For easy construction, the sashing pieces are stitched to each quilt block. When the framed blocks are stitched together, the sashing forms an eight-pointed star where the corners of four blocks meet, and the pieced triangles form squares in the design.

The unpieced quilt blocks, cut from a single fabric, may be embellished with quilting or appliqués. The sashing is constructed from gradations of a color. The choice of color in the sashing can create either a subtle frame around each block or a bold design.

The instructions that follow are for a bed quilt. For a twin-size, which measures about 68" × 86" (173 × 218.5 cm), three rows of two blocks are pieced. For a full/queen-size, which measures about 86" (218.5 cm) square, three rows of three blocks are pieced. The sashing is constructed around 12" (30.5 cm) quilt blocks. Each block framed with

3" (7.5 cm) sashing measures 18" (46 cm) square. Wide 16" (40.5 cm) borders complete the quilt and provide a background for decorative quilting. To eliminate the need for piecing, the border strips are cut on the lengthwise grain.

✀ Cutting Directions

Cut two 3½" (9 cm) strips of each of the eight solid-colored fabrics for sashing; these will be cut into parallelograms (page 110).

Cut the four fabrics for sashing triangles into 7¼" (18.7 cm) squares; for a twin-size quilt, cut two squares of each fabric, and for a full/queen-size quilt, cut three squares of each fabric. Cut all squares diagonally in both directions (page 13), making four triangles from each square.

For the quilt blocks, cut 12½" (31.8 cm) fabric strips; cut the strips into squares, cutting six for a twin-size quilt and nine for a full/queen-size.

YOU WILL NEED

For twin-size:

¾ yd. (0.7 m) fabric, to be used for quilt blocks.

¼ yd. (0.25 m) each of eight solid-colored fabrics for sashing parallelograms; choose eight shades of one color.

Scraps or ¼ yd. (0.25 m) each of four fabrics for sashing triangles.

3¾ yd. (3.45 m) fabric, to be used for continuous-length 16" (40.5 cm) borders.

2¾ yd. (2.55 m) fabric in 90" (229 cm) width, or 5¼ yd. (4.8 m) in 45" (115 cm) width, for backing.

¾ yd. (0.7 m) fabric for binding.

Batting, sized for twin-size quilt.

For full/queen-size:

1⅛ yd. (1.05 m) fabric, to be used for quilt blocks.

¼ yd. (0.25 m) each of eight solid-colored fabrics for sashing parallelograms; choose eight shades of one color.

Scraps or ¼ yd. (0.25 m) each of four fabrics for sashing triangles.

4¼ yd. (3.9 m) fabric, to be used for continuous-length 16" (40.5 cm) borders.

2¾ yd. (2.55 m) fabric in 108" (274.5 cm) width, or 7¾ yd. (7.1 m) in 45" (115 cm) width, for backing.

¾ yd. (0.7 m) fabric for binding.

Batting, sized for full/queen-size quilt.

How to Make a Quilt with Frame Sashing

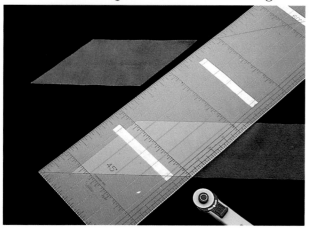

1) **Cut** a 45° angle on one end of strip for sashing. Place 4¾" (12 cm) mark of ruler along angled cut; cut strip to make parallelogram.

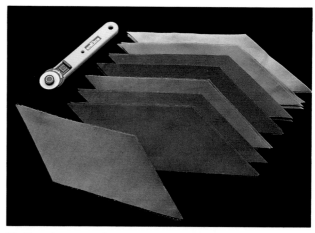

2) **Continue** cutting parallelograms from fabric strips, cutting six of each fabric for twin-size or nine of each fabric for full/queen-size.

3) **Stitch** two parallelograms of different colors to short sides of one triangle, as shown; finger-press seam allowances toward parallelograms. Trim points that extend beyond sashing.

4) **Repeat** step 3 to make four pieced sashing strips for each quilt block; randomly use each parallelogram and triangle fabric once in each set.

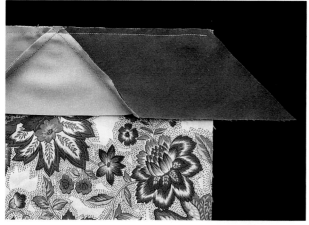

5) **Stitch** short side of one pieced sashing strip to one side of quilt block; begin and end stitching ¼" (6 mm) from edges of block, backstitching at ends. Repeat for remaining sides of block.

6) **Fold** quilt block diagonally, right sides together, matching seamlines and edges of parallelograms.

7) Stitch corner seam, backstitching at inside corner; do not catch seam allowances in stitching. Repeat for remaining corners.

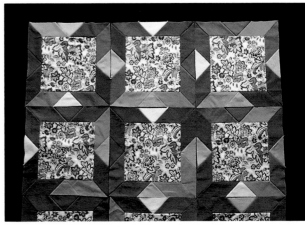

8) Repeat steps 5 to 7 for remaining blocks, varying color arrangement. Arrange blocks in rows.

9) Stitch blocks into rows, matching points; stitch rows together, finger-pressing seam allowances at corners in opposite directions. Press the quilt top, pressing seam allowances toward blocks.

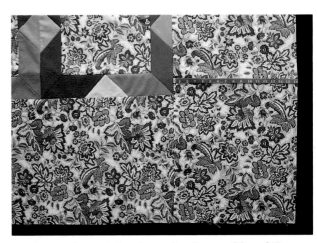

10) Cut and attach border strips (pages 20 to 25), cutting strips on lengthwise grain; cut width of border strips is 16½" (41.8 cm). Mark quilting design on border and blocks (page 30).

11) Cut backing and batting about 4" (10 cm) larger than quilt top. Layer and baste quilt top, batting, and backing (pages 26 and 27).

12) Quilt (pages 28 to 35). Cut and apply binding (page 37); cut width of binding is 2½" (6.5 cm).

Star Sashing

Sashing strips with connecting stars create a sashing design bold enough to be used with plain quilt blocks. Quick methods for cutting and piecing are used to construct the stars, making this an easy quilt project.

The instructions that follow are for a quilt made from thirty 5½" (14 cm) quilt blocks and 2¼" (6 cm) sashing. The finished quilt with a double lapped border measures about 45" × 53" (115 × 134.5 cm).

✂ Cutting Directions

Cut eight 2¾" (7 cm) strips from the fabric for the sashing strips, and cut the strips into forty-nine 6" (15 cm) rectangles. Cut two 2¾" (7 cm) strips from the fabric for the stars; cut into twenty 2¾" (7 cm) squares. Cut seven 1⅝" (4 cm) strips from the fabric for the stars; cut into 160 squares to be used for the points of the stars. For the quilt blocks, cut five 6" (15 cm) fabric strips; cut into 30 squares.

YOU WILL NEED

1 yd. (0.95 m) fabric for quilt blocks.

⅞ yd. ((0.8 m) fabric for sashing strips.

⅔ yd. (0.63 m) fabric for stars and ½" (1.3 cm) inner border.

¾ yd. (0.7 m) fabric for 3½" (9 cm) outer border.

½ yd. (0.5 m) fabric for binding.

2¾ yd. (2.55 m) fabric for backing.

Batting, about 49" × 57" (125 × 144.5 cm).

How to Make a Quilt with Star Sashing

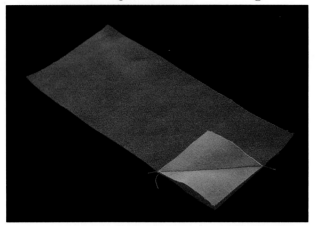

1) Place 1⅝" (4 cm) square in one corner of sashing strip, with right sides together and raw edges even. Stitch diagonally as shown.

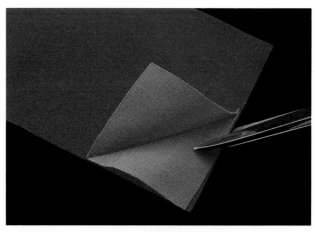

2) Press square in half along stitched line, matching outer edges to sashing strip. Trim fabric at stitched corner, leaving ¼" (6 mm) seam allowance.

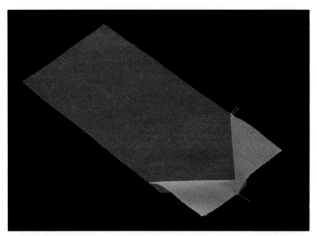

3) Repeat steps 1 and 2 at opposite corner. Continue piecing squares at one end of rectangles for a total of 18 pieced strips; these will be used as end strips.

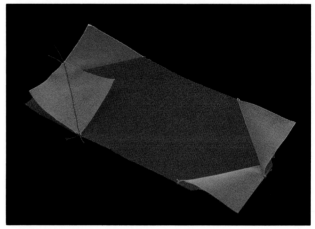

4) Stitch squares to all four corners of remaining sashing strips; these will be used as inner strips.

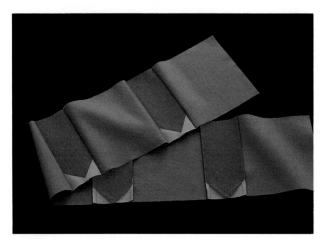

5) Stitch four end strips between five quilt blocks, placing plain ends at upper edge; this will be top row of quilt. Press seam allowances toward blocks.

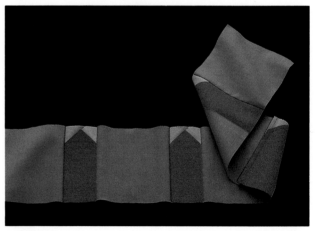

6) Repeat step 5 to make a second row, placing plain ends at lower edge; this will be bottom row of quilt.

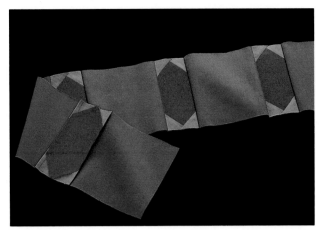

7) Stitch four inner strips between five quilt blocks to make one of the middle rows. Press seam allowances toward blocks. Repeat for three more rows.

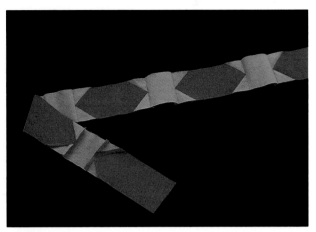

8) Stitch five sashing strips alternately to the sashing squares, using an end strip at each end. Press seam allowances toward squares. Repeat for four more rows.

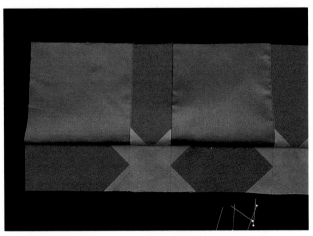

9) Pin one sashing unit along bottom of top row, right sides together, matching seams; stitch. Repeat for remaining rows, except for bottom row.

10) Pin bottom of one sashing unit to top of next row, matching seams; stitch. Continue until all rows are joined. Press seam allowances toward sashing.

11) Cut and attach border strips (pages 20 to 25); cut width of border strips is 1" (2.5 cm) for inner border and 4" (10 cm) for outer border. Cut backing 4" (10 cm) larger than quilt top. Layer and baste quilt top, batting, and backing (pages 26 and 27).

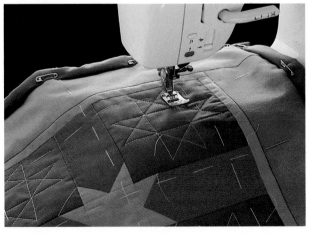

12) Quilt (pages 28 to 35). Cut and apply binding (page 37); cut width of binding is 2½" (6.5 cm). For wall hanging, apply fabric sleeve (page 39).

More Star Sashing Designs

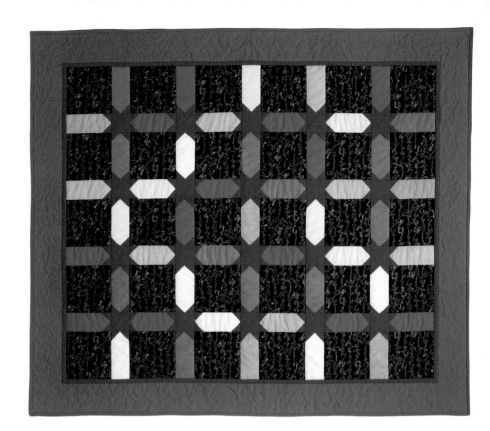

Add variety to star sashing by piecing each star in a different color or by using a gradation of colors for the sashing strips. Or for a more intricate design, use strip-pieced sashing. When using a variety of fabrics, make a sketch of the quilt for easier cutting and assembly.

Gradated colors are used for the sashing strips in the quilt at right to add subtle interest to the design.

Bright stars in a rainbow of colors are used for this child's quilt. The multicolored printed fabric in the quilt blocks adds interest to the quilt. A brightly colored stripe is used for one of the fabrics in the triple border.

Calicos and plaids create a traditional look, with template-quilted blocks complementing the style. The sashing has been strip-pieced for a more intricate design.

Dark and jewel-tone fabrics create an Amish-style quilt. Strip-pieced sashing adds more interest.

How to Make Strip-pieced Star Sashing

1) Cut fabric strips on crosswise grain 1¼" (3.2 cm) wide, cutting three for each row of sashing. Stitch strips together lengthwise in desired sequence, right sides together. Press.

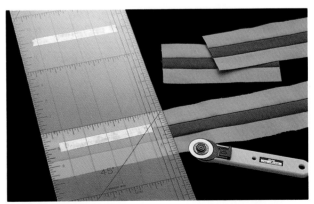

2) Cut pieced fabric into 6" (15 cm) rectangles for sashing strips. Make quilt as on pages 112 to 115.

Strip-pieced Sashing

Sashing with connecting squares gives a quilt an updated look when strip-pieced from gradated fabrics. Connecting squares in a bold contrasting color add another design element.

You may want to select a printed fabric for the quilt blocks and choose colors from that fabric to use for the gradation and connecting squares; the sharper the contrast, the bolder the design will be.

The instructions that follow are for a wall hanging made from nine 8" (20.5 cm) quilt blocks and 2" (5 cm) sashing. Random quilting lines complement the style of the quilt and create interest in the center of the quilt where the lines intersect. Instead of the

narrow binding that is usually used on small wall hangings, the traditional binding acts as a small border. The finished project measures about 32" (81.5 cm) square.

✄ Cutting Directions

Cut 1½" (3.8 cm) strips from each gradated color for sashing strips; cut four strips of each color from fat quarters or two strips from 45" (115 cm) yardage. Cut one 2½" (6.5 cm) fabric strip from the fabric for the connecting squares; cut the strip into sixteen 2½" (6.5 cm) squares. For the quilt blocks, cut two 8½" (21.8 cm) fabric strips; cut into nine 8½" (21.8 cm) squares.

YOU WILL NEED

⅛ yd. (0.15 m) each of eight fabrics, or one packet of hand-dyed fabrics in fat quarters, for sashing.

⅛ yd. (0.15 m) fabric for connecting squares.

¾ yd. (0.7 m) printed fabric for quilt blocks.

⅓ yd. (0.32 m) fabric for binding.

1 yd. (0.95 m) fabric for backing.

Batting, about 36" (91.5 cm) square.

How to Make a Quilt with Gradated Sashing

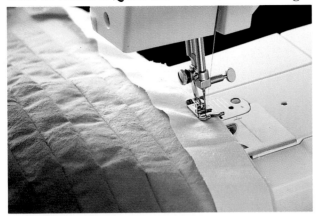

1) Stitch one strip of each color together lengthwise, with right sides together and in gradated sequence; repeat for remaining strips. Press seam allowances in one direction.

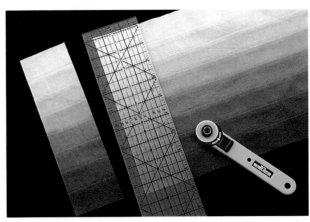

2) Cut the pieced fabric crosswise into 2½" (6.5 cm) strips, using rotary cutter.

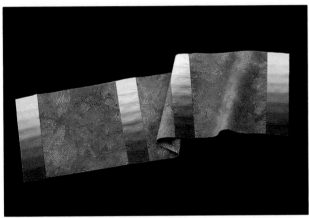

3) Stitch pieced strips between blocks, to form three rows of three blocks, with darkest color at bottom of quilt blocks; stitch pieced strips to ends of rows. Press seam allowances toward blocks.

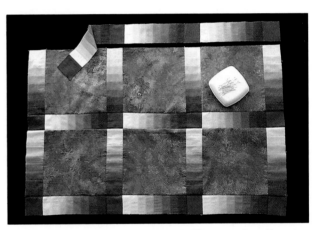

4) Complete sashing, as on page 19, steps 3 to 5; arrange strips as shown.

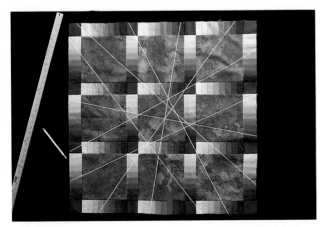

5) Mark quilting lines (page 30); draw lines randomly across quilt top, drawing about four lines from each side. Layer and baste quilt top, batting, and backing fabric (pages 26 and 27). (Markings were exaggerated for clarity.)

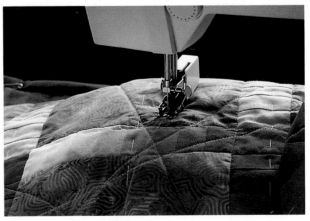

6) Quilt along sashing as on pages 34 and 35, using stitch-in-the-ditch method; then quilt on marked lines. Cut and apply binding (page 37); cut width of binding is 2½" (6.5 cm). For wall hanging, attach fabric sleeve (page 39).

More Strip-pieced Sashing Designs

For more colorful designs, piece fabric strips from gradated blends of two or more colors. Or cut the connecting squares from several colors. To create more motion in the quilt design, vary the arrangement of the sashing strips.

Gradated strips are arranged in the quilt at right so the dark and light colors alternately radiate from connecting squares.

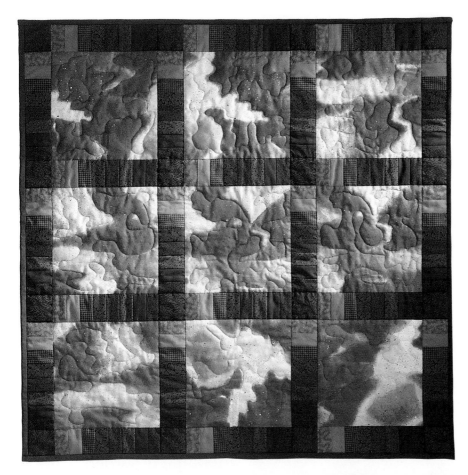

Printed fabrics in blended colors are used for the pieced sashing in the quilt at left. The blocks have been quilted, using free-motion quilting, to enhance the design of the mottled fabric.

Rainbow colors in the sashing are used with solid-colored blocks to make the quilt shown below. The blocks are embellished with template quilting.

Creative Borders

Borders, such as the appliquéd border shown here, can become an integral and important part of the quilt design instead of merely a frame for the quilt. Or borders can add an unexpected finishing touch, as shown on the quilts on pages 124 and 125.

Appliquéd Borders

An asymmetrical border, applied as an overlay, adds interest to a quilt. The edges of the border are appliquéd to the quilt top, following the design of the fabric. The border can provide a strong contrast to the pieced top or can blend subtly.

An appliquéd border may be added to as many sides of the quilt as desired. When planning the border, you may want to make a sketch of the quilt, or lay strips of the border fabric on the pieced quilt top to determine the desired size of the border pieces.

For the border, choose a printed fabric that can be cut and pressed along a design line. The yardage requirements will vary, depending on the size of the quilt and the width of the border strips. Estimate the yardage for the border as on page 20; for best results, plan for continuous border strips. When cutting the strips, you may want to allow extra width on the appliquéd borders to allow for adjusting the placement of the design line.

YOU WILL NEED

Printed fabric for appliquéd border, yardage determined as at right.

Fabric for narrow outer border, yardage determined as on page 20.

Pieced quilt top in desired quilt design.

Backing, yardage determined as on page 26.

Batting, about 4" (10 cm) larger than quilt top.

How to Apply an Appliquéd Border

1) Press quilt top. Measure side, or portion of side, to be covered by first border strip. Cut the length of border strip to this measurement; cut width is equal to desired depth at widest point plus ½" (1.3 cm). Mark inner edge of border strip along design line.

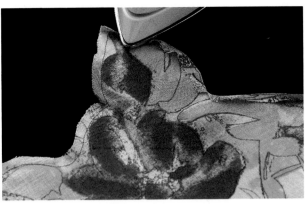

2) Stitch on the marked lines; trim ¼" (6 mm) from the stitching. Press under edge of fabric just beyond stitching line; clip as necessary.

3) Pin border strip to quilt top, making sure the edges overlap and the corners are squared with the quilt. Blindstitch along pressed edges as on page 78, step 4. Trim excess fabric from wrong side, allowing ¼" (6 mm) seam allowance.

4) Measure adjacent side, or portion of that side, to be covered by second border strip. Cut the length of second strip to this measurement plus extra to overlap first strip; cut width is equal to desired depth at widest point plus ½" (1.3 cm). Mark inner edge of strip.

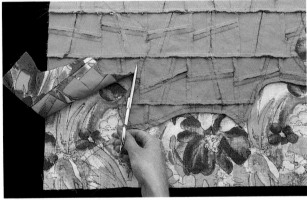

5) Stitch and press inner edge of second border strip as in step 2. Pin and blindstitch border as in step 3; trim excess fabric from wrong side, allowing ¼" (6 mm) seam allowance. Apply any remaining border strips as for second strip.

6) Cut and attach outer border, if desired (pages 20 to 25). Cut backing about 4" (10 cm) larger than quilt top. Layer and baste quilt top, batting, and backing (pages 26 and 27). Quilt (pages 28 to 35). Cut and apply binding (page 37). For wall hanging, attach fabric sleeve (page 39).

Randomly pieced border adds a creative frame to this table runner with satin-stiched appliqués (pages 80 and 81).

More Creative Border Designs

A creative border adds a new area of interest to a quilt, instead of a simple, complementary frame. The border can emphasize the colors used in piecing and can change the balance of the quilt.

Randomly pieced borders can incorporate fabrics that are too overpowering to use as continuous strips. Piece scraps together for the necessary yardage for the border strips.

Another way to incorporate several fabrics is by applying multiple borders. Instead of the usual single or double borders, several borders may be used on one quilt.

Unbalanced borders are especially pleasing on wall hangings. An unbalanced border creates motion in the quilt design, making the quilt more interesting when viewed from a distance.

Mitered border is applied to two sides only. The Pine Trees quilt (page 43) is displayed on point, with the top hanging free to reveal the quilt's patterned backing.

Bias tape is gently curved along the border of the contemporary crazy quilt (page 91) shown at left. Use the machine blindstitch to apply the bias tape, as on page 78.

Multiple borders of various colors and widths, shown below on a string-pieced quilt (page 95), were applied using the method for lapped borders (pages 20 to 22). The inner, or first, border is entirely red. The second and third borders are each half blue and half purple. The fourth partial border, applied only to the top and left side, repeats the red.

Contrasting insert strips make a contemporary frame for a landscape wall hanging (page 100); add the strips to the border as on page 88. Start by applying the border strip on the left side of the quilt; then work counterclockwise, and miter the upper left corner.

Index

Creative Publishing international, Inc.
offers a variety of how-to books. For
information write:
  Creative Publishing international, Inc.
  Subscriber Books
  18705 Lake Drive East
  Chanhassen, MN 55317